PITTSYLVANIA COUNTY

——— AND THE ———

WAR OF 1812

LARRY G. AARON

To Vic Millner

FOREWORD BY STUART BUTLER

*Friend and fellow member
of the Pittsylvania County
War of 1812 Bicentennial
Committee.*

Larry G Aaron

December 15, 2014

THE
History
PRESS

Published by The History Press
Charleston, SC 29403
www.historypress.net

Cover images: Top image, left to right: Rachel Jackson, Walker Coles, Dolley Madison. Bottom image: *Painful March of Volunteers*, engraving from *The Second War with England*, by J.T. Headley.

First published 2014

Manufactured in the United States

ISBN 978.1.62619.750.3

Library of Congress Control Number: 2014953172

*To Walter Coles V of Coles Hill,
Pittsylvania County, Virginia.*

CONTENTS

FOREWORD

The War of 1812—or, as the British referred to it at the time, the American War—is probably the least understood and most "forgotten" war in American history. Yet so many of our most patriotic sayings and slogans came out of this war. Stirring statements such as "Don't give up the ship!" and "We have met the enemy and they are ours" derive from both our naval success and failures during the war. Not to mention "The Star-Spangled Banner," sung perhaps hundreds if not thousands of times by Americans on a daily basis.

The recent spate of publications about the war from both sides of the Atlantic has helped Americans to better understand the origins and legacy of the war. This is in no small part due to the commemoration of the 200th anniversary of the War of 1812. Primarily observed in those states in which events took place, many of these observances have taken place on local or state levels. Most Americans, if at all familiar with the War of 1812, probably know about the burning of the Capitol and the White House in Washington, D.C.; the repulse of the British at Baltimore; and Andrew Jackson's great victory over the British at New Orleans. However, many Americans, in particular Virginians, would be surprised to learn that Virginia suffered more from British depredations and raids during the war than any other state, with the exception of New York and possibly Maryland. British naval forces remained in Virginia's waters longer than in any other state's. From that presence in February 1813 until March 1815, British naval and marine forces launched punishing raids on small towns and plantations up and down the Chesapeake Bay.

Larry Aaron, in his *Pittsylvania County and the War of 1812*, reminds us that there is much to be learned through regional studies. Aaron points out that since there was no British presence in Pittsylvania County during the war, the county, in response to Governor James Barbour's call for help, sent many of its local militia to defend the commonwealth from British incursions. Aaron tells us that many of the men were sent to Norfolk during the course of the war. Norfolk was the chief port for Virginia, and its capture or destruction by the British would have been devastating to the war effort if not to the trade and commerce of the rest of Virginia and northeastern North Carolina. Others, he notes, were sent to Richmond camps to deter possible British invasion along the James River. As the threat to Richmond subsided in September 1814, several Pittsylvania County companies were diverted from Richmond to the Washington-Baltimore area, eventually camping at Ellicott's Mill, just outside Baltimore, until the end of November.

Using the invaluable records at the National Archives and Records Administration and other depositories, Aaron is able to record the movements and experiences of a number of Pittsylvania soldiers during the war. He makes judicious use of the personal information about militia soldiers from pension and bounty land application files that the soldiers or their families obtained from the U.S. government after the war. Pittsylvanians also enlisted and served in the regular U.S. Army during the war. From official and personal letters found in archives, libraries and in private hands, Aaron highlights the army career of Captain Walter Coles. In letters to his sister back in Pittsylvania, Captain Coles described his military life and service, particularly its hardships, on the Canadian frontier.

Larry Aaron's book makes a fine contribution to the growing number of new publications on the War of 1812. In doing so, he emphasizes the local aspect of the war and how one rural Virginia county was affected by the war, as well as the contributions of its citizens to the greater war effort. We need more books like Mr. Aaron's to help tell the full story of Virginia's role in the war.

Stuart Butler

ACKNOWLEDGEMENTS

A book of this sort is hardly the sole work of one individual, and so it is in this case. Without the contributions of others, this story of Pittsylvania County and the War of 1812 could not have been written.

First and foremost, I dedicate this book to Walter Coles V of Coles Hill in Pittsylvania County, whose ancestor Walter Coles I served in the U.S. Army during the War of 1812. Walter V grew up on a tobacco and cattle farm in the Pittsylvania plantation home built by his ancestor in 1815 shortly after the war. After graduating from The Citadel in South Carolina, Walter embarked on a distinguished army career, with two tours of duty in the Vietnam War, during which he received Bronze Stars for ground operation against hostile forces and Air Medals for distinguished service in aerial flight operations over enemy territory.

Following Vietnam, he served thirty years as a career diplomat in the U.S. Foreign Service as an economic development officer, the "key architect for U.S. policy initiatives on privatization and land reform implementation" in former Soviet bloc countries. He was especially honored by the president of Moldova for his extraordinary assistance in transforming that country's economy.

For this work, Walter V generously provided letters from his 1812 ancestor Walter Coles I, whose writings home—along with those of his cousin, Elbridge Gerry Jr., of Boston to his sister, Catherine Coles, of Pittsylvania County—revealed a great deal about the war on the Canadian frontier, as well as military life. Due to the scarcity of 1812 letters from soldiers, these letters make the war a more personable story while at the same time adding exciting new information about the War of 1812.

Copies of original letters from Walter Coles I and Elbridge Gerry Jr. in the Papers of the Gerry and Coles Families at the Huntington Library in San Marino, California, were acquired with the help of Olga Tsapina, Norris Foundation curator of American history.

Secondly, I would like to thank the Pittsylvania Historical Society for awarding me a grant from the Herman and Helen Melton Historical Fund, which is dedicated to historical research and preservation in Pittsylvania County. Herman Melton, now deceased, wrote a short letter to me at the beginning of this project, congratulating me on having received the grant that he and his wife endowed. His words kept me going. He noted that little attention had been paid to this subject in Pittsylvania County histories and added, "The project is long overdue...It's time somebody did [it]." I was honored to have his blessing and only wish that he could have lived to see the finished product.

I especially want to mention fellow society board members Charles Strauss, retired Virginia Circuit Court judge; Vic Milner, a distinguished Chatham attorney; and William Black, Professor Emeritus of Chatham Hall. The four of us composed the Pittsylvania County Bicentennial Committee of the War of 1812, which was established to commemorate this 200th anniversary of the conflict. Their encouragement in the writing of this book turned this project into a mission to educate the local community about the importance of this war.

Desiree Berrios assisted me with significant research for this project through her public history internship from Longwood University under the auspices of the Pittsylvania Historical Society. Her analysis of War of 1812 records related to Pittsylvania County was an essential part of this project.

Stuart Butler, *the* authority on the War of 1812 in Virginia and author of *Defending the Old Dominion: A Guide to Virginia Militia Units in the War of 1812* and other like publications on the war, could not have been more helpful. A former National Archivist in Washington, Stuart graciously provided research material, answered numerous questions, provided editorial advice and honored this endeavor by agreeing to write the foreword. His books are indispensable in studying the War of 1812 in Virginia, and I have made use of his research throughout this book.

Chris Hanks of Pittsylvaniacountyhistory.com provided me with copies of pension records from the National Archives in Washington, along with information from his website about graves of War of 1812 veterans. His contribution of research material not only was generous but also made this work measurably more than what it would have been.

Then, too, Mike Lyman of the Society of the War of 1812 in Virginia also provided information about cemeteries in Virginia and especially those in Pittsylvania County where soldiers of that war were buried. His book *Encounters with the British in Virginia during the War of 1812* is an outstanding resource, and a study of the war in Virginia would not be complete without it.

For contributing images, copies and/or other information related to their Pittsylvania County ancestors' service during the War of 1812, I want to thank Betty Camp; Ginger Gentry; Mary Catherine Plaster; Glenn Giles; Vernell Gwyn; my cousin Marvin Osborne; Mike Geisinger; Melissa Sims Hairston and her father, Bob Sims; Linda Burger; and Kevin Bowers and Chuck Walters, both descendants of Lieutenant Colonel Daniel Coleman's family.

Others contributed articles, books, documentation of various kinds and research information: Henry Hurt, former *Reader's Digest* editor of Chatham, Virginia; local historian and author Lawrence McFall of Danville, Virginia; Barbara Bass, president of the Halifax County Historical Society; Juliette Arai of the Archive Reference Section at the National Archives; Geoffrey Skelly of the University of Virginia Center for Politics; Kurt Cederquist of DigiGraphics in Minneapolis, Minnesota; Dr. Rick Dixon, social studies teacher and department chair of Modern and Classical Languages at the Episcopal High School in Alexandria, Virginia; Sarah Mitchell, former editor of the *Pittsylvania Packet*; Pittsylvania County school librarian Robert Joyce; and Ophelia Payne of the University of Virginia Digitization Services.

My research took me to the Alderman Library and the Albert and Shirley Small Special Collections Library, both at the University of Virginia; the Davis Library at the University of North Carolina; the Library of Virginia at Richmond; and the genealogical section of the Danville Public Library, administered by the Virginia–North Carolina Genealogical Society. The National Archives and Records Administration and the Library of Congress were both sources of information and imagery. The Internet site Ancestry.com was especially useful in accessing military records. Also, the Bureau of Land Management was the source for bounty land certificates relating to the War of 1812.

And I would not want to leave out others who have assisted me in small ways from time to time: Liz Robertson, corresponding secretary of the Virginia–North Carolina Genealogical Society; Nina Thornton and

Frances Haley, colleagues and fellow travelers; longtime friend Ron Francis of the Pittsylvania County History Center; and Angie Harris, secretary to Pittsylvania Circuit Court judge Stacey Moreau.

I should also thank my son, John Mark Aaron, who contributed technological support when my computer seemed to develop a mind of its own during the preparation of this manuscript. Neither should I forget my dear wife, Nancy, whose understanding and patience allowed me time to work on this manuscript while my "Honey-Do" list lapsed into overtime neglect.

Finally, I thank my commissioning editor at The History Press, Banks Smither, for his enthusiasm for this project and his patience while guiding me through the publication process. In addition, copyeditor Ryan Finn at The History Press made valuable suggestions and corrections to the manuscript.

INTRODUCTION

In America, we sing about the War of 1812 more than any other war. We pledge allegiance to the flag and hear the words of "The Star-Spangled Banner" echo through standing crowds at public rallies and sports events. Yet we sing a glorious tribute to a war about which most Americans know little.

The War of 1812 has been called the "forgotten war," but it is a war we need to study, relive and digest because it was a turning point in the affairs of this nation. Historian Ralph Eshelman, in *Bay Journeys*, pointed out that "[p]rior to the war you would have said, 'The United States are.' After the war, you would have said, 'The United States is.'" As a result of the War of 1812, America *became* the motto inscribed on the national seal of the United States: *E pluribus unum* ("Out of many, one"). The Revolutionary War gave us independence; the War of 1812 made us a nation.

No one would have expected such a result. It was a short war and a strange one. It was the first foreign war that our nation entered into after the Revolution of 1776 and the most divisive war in our history, more so than the war in Vietnam. It was a war practically nobody wanted, yet it happened anyway. And we were totally unprepared when we declared war against an enemy supremely more powerful than ourselves. As the war progressed, it appeared to be a disaster in the making. Almost anything that could go wrong did.

It was a battle of unequal proportions if ever there was one. It was the biblical David with hardly a stone to throw against Goliath, the British empire. There were easy predictions about America defeating Great Britain, but they quickly faded into the darkness of reality. And yet, looking back at the war during its 200th anniversary, the conflict almost seemed necessary. It was time for America to cut the apron strings and invent its future. And like a great movie, it had a surprise ending, albeit one that had little to do with the reasons for going to war.

Understanding how the war played out and how its impact continues into today's scientific and technologically advanced world is important for each of us as we exercise our roles as citizens having a voice in the direction of this country. As Marcus Tullius Cicero expressed it, "Not to know what happened before you were born is to remain forever a child." We cannot be ignorant of the history of our country and expect to be good citizens.

What happened during the War of 1812 is also important because it is part of our personal past, and that connection to the past has everything to do with who we are and what we are about. In a real sense, we are part of our nation's history, having had it bequeathed to us by our forefathers.

But the war is also a legacy to guide our economic and political policies into the third millennium. George Santayana is famous for the quote, "Those who cannot remember the past are doomed to repeat it." Great lessons were learned in the War of 1812, lessons that are still relevant for America today. It almost goes without saying that lessons learned must always be in our rear-view mirror as our country readjusts to its place in this changing world.

Fitting the story of Pittsylvania County soldiers into the context of the War of 1812 brings the war home to the local level. The truth is that all history is local history. America's history is local history on a grand scale.

In the pages that follow, the reader will connect with events from America's pre-revolutionary days, continue through the administration of President Washington to that of President James Madison during the war and, finally, catch a glimpse of the "Era of Good Feelings" afterward. Some of those events affecting our nation before, during and after the war also affected Pittsylvania County economically, politically and militarily.

While the war might seem a bit foggy and dull history, it has all the drama one could ask for. It gave us five U.S. presidents and a host of heroes, including a president's wife. The country received iconic symbols in a ship, a flag and that song that's heard every day somewhere in America.

In addition to the story of the war itself, the reader will find unpublished images and information from letters, pensions, bounty land applications and other documents related to Pittsylvania County during the war.

Although Pittsylvania County was far from the scenes of battle in that war, some of its soldiers in the U.S. Army served on battlefronts in the Canadian campaigns along the northern border. But the war was not just in some faraway place. It happened here in Virginia, too. And of those who rallied to Virginia's defense, not a few were from Pittsylvania County. Just as their fathers and grandfathers had fought in the American Revolution to give America the liberties expounded in the Declaration of Independence, during the War of 1812 the next generation of patriots from Pittsylvania County joined in their country's struggle to maintain those liberties. This is their story.

Chapter 1

UNFINISHED BUSINESS

The War of 1812 really started before the ink was dry on the 1783 Treaty of Paris that ended the American Revolution.
—U.S. Navy captain Wilbur Sundt, Naval Science

In 1790, the American Revolution was thought to be over. The United States had a constitution, and George Washington was president. In Pittsylvania County, Virginia, lots of available land, coupled with migration from the coastal regions, kept this rural county growing. Pittsylvania County enjoyed a significant population in 1790, with nearly twelve thousand inhabitants.

Although the county was situated far inland at the edge of the Blue Ridge and somewhat isolated from the centers of commerce, major ports and the business of the national government, its connection with the outside world wasn't limited. The county exchanged its tobacco for merchandise and supplies from the mother country, England. Otherwise, it probably had little involvement with the international arena, where simmering events would soon boil over, embroiling the county in a second war of independence.

However, as a small section of a new republic trying to find its way in the world, Pittsylvania's isolated location in the backwater of Virginia likely prohibited its inhabitants from envisioning the country's place on the world stage. Pittsylvania County would have been more concerned about settling the land, building new homes, rearing families and working the farms. The county certainly wasn't thinking about war again with England.

But George Washington saw something coming. As the first president of the United States ended his second term of office in 1796, he wrote a "Farewell Address" to the American people, raising concerns about issues that would become problematic during the War of 1812. Among those issues were sectionalism, the spirit of party and permanent alliances with foreign nations, especially those in Europe.

Mounting controversy had developed between different political philosophies, not unlike those that fueled the earlier debate over the ratification of the Constitution. These different views of government helped create two political parties that thoroughly opposed each other.

The Federalists believed in a strong central government with an aggressive commercial economy. Alexander Hamilton, first secretary of the treasury, proposed a national bank that would help facilitate commerce and allow the government to fund its operations. Sources of revenue would consist of taxes and tariffs on imports. The Federalists believed that America should become, as Alan Brinkley wrote in *The Unfinished Nation*, "a nation with a wealthy, enlightened ruling class, a vigorous, independent commercial economy, and a thriving manufacturing sector."

Thomas Jefferson, the nation's first secretary of state, and James Madison, who would lead the nation during the War of 1812, both embraced what became the Democratic-Republican outlook. They did not see America as an industrial or manufacturing empire. As Eric Foner noted in *Give Me Liberty*, "Jefferson and Madison concluded that the greatest threat to American freedom lay in the alliance of a powerful central government with an emerging class of commercial capitalists." In Jefferson's words, "Were I to indulge my own theory, I should wish them [the states] to practice neither commerce nor navigation [shipping]."

Neither did Jefferson or his followers want any part of a national bank. It smacked of opportunities for corruption and control of the nation's money by the powerful. The nation's first national bank had a twenty-year charter that expired in 1811 during Jefferson's administration and was not renewed until after the War of 1812.

Jefferson's vision of America was an agricultural republic of farmers marketing their products to the world at large. He wrote, "Those who labor in the earth are the chosen people of God, if ever he had a chosen people, whose breasts he has made his peculiar deposit for substantial and genuine virtue." That vision of America resonated well in Pittsylvania County, with its growing agricultural community.

With the westward expansion of the country, especially after the Louisiana Purchase of 1803, land would be available for agricultural pursuits, and the sale of those lands would help finance the government. Also, customs duties on imports would supply the remainder of America's financial needs. Eric Foner argued that "[Jefferson and Madison] had little desire to promote manufacturing or urban growth or to see economic policy shaped in the interests of bankers and business leaders." Consequently, when Jefferson became president in 1800, he convinced Congress to abolish all internal taxes, believing that revenue could be accumulated without resorting to commercial enterprise. Unfortunately, the coming war with Britain and the loss of trade incurred by it led the country into financial difficulty.

Also, during the War of 1812, the lack of a national bank made it difficult for the country to borrow money to finance the war. Most of the nation's mercantile and financial resources were from New Jersey northward, and northern merchants and state banks, mostly in Federalist-dominated New England, refused to loan money to the government.

Additionally, Jefferson, a believer in limited government, pared down its size to reduce spending. In the process, he also reduced the size of the army to 2,500 men and the navy from twenty-five ships to seven. A large standing army and navy brought up past fears of when the British used them against the colonists. This, too, would be problematic in the coming war.

So, there existed side by side two different views about America that conflicted severely. And the conflict of ideas was all about what union meant and what America was to become. The Federalists mostly aligned themselves with Great Britain and its model of centralized authority, while believing that government by the masses, as demonstrated by the French Revolution, would lead to anarchy.

The Democratic-Republican Party, as it was known then (the ancestor of our present Democratic Party), tended to look to France as its inspiration. Jefferson, America's first minister to France, received his political beliefs about the natural rights of man—in part embodied in the Declaration of Independence—from the French Enlightenment. That philosophy was based on faith in nature and reason, resulting in government by people not by monarchs or powerful heads of state who ruled arbitrarily. As a result, the French Revolution dethroned King Louis XVI, and the people adopted the principles of freedom, equality and brotherhood—that is, they adopted a form of government that did not involve obedience to a monarch such as George III of Great Britain.

Both the Federalist and Republican political viewpoints, and their alignment with Britain and France, respectively, erupted into issues that fueled the debate over the War of 1812, propelled the nation into that war and played out during the war until the end.

Pittsylvania County's citizens, like many in the agricultural South, heavily supported Jefferson and Madison's approach to government. In the presidential election of 1804 in Virginia, every Republican elector for Thomas Jefferson received all 358 votes from Pittsylvania County; Federalist electors received none. In the election for president in 1808, the Republican electors received 245 votes for James Madison, while the Federalist electors received 7. In 1812, after the war began, Madison ran for president again, and his electors received 153 votes, while the Federalist electors got only 15. Although a smaller margin than before, Pittsylvania County also joined the rest of the South in supporting Madison.

But it might be added that Pittsylvania County had close connections with President Madison. Elbridge Gerry Sr. of Massachusetts, a signer of the Declaration of Independence and former governor of Massachusetts, was Madison's vice president in his second term. His son, Elbridge Gerry Jr., was first cousin to Walter Coles of Coles Hill in Pittsylvania County, Virginia, since their mothers were sisters.

In Elbridge Gerry Jr.'s diary, written when he stayed with his father in Washington in the winter of 1813, he told of visiting President and Mrs. Madison at the President's House:

> *I sat with Mrs. Madison all the eve and found her of elegant manners, accomplished and easy, and at the same time, possessed of that pleasing dignity which will always command the esteem and respect of every person. She treated me with friendly attention, and more like a son than a stranger…I was soon informed by her that I was second cousin to her.*

At one point in the diary, Elbridge Jr. wrote that his father introduced him to "Col. Coles, who I found to be my cousin." That would have been Isaac Coles, the father of Lieutenant Walter Coles, who at that time was serving in the war. Walter Coles and Dolley Madison were also second cousins, since her grandfather William Coles and his grandfather John Coles were brothers.

While most of New England was of the Federalist persuasion, Elbridge Gerry Sr. was not. Although he supported the economic policies of Federalist Alexander Hamilton, he also became an advocate of war with

Left: Walter Coles I, son of Isaac Coles of Pittsylvania County, served in the War of 1812 during the campaigns along the Canadian border. *Walter Coles V Collection.*

Right: Elbridge Gerry Sr., whose wife, Ann Thompson, was the aunt of Captain Walter Coles of Pittsylvania County, Virginia; Gerry Sr. was a signer of the Declaration of Independence, governor of Massachusetts and vice president of the United States under President James Madison. *Library of Congress.*

Great Britain. However strong his influence might have been in New England, the Federalist influence was stronger, and Gerry Sr. was definitely in the minority there.

Besides the Federalist versus Republican political divide, another internal issue in which Pittsylvania County would find itself involved—one that spilled over into the War of 1812—was what to do about continued migration of settlers into Indian lands. This was an issue that had developed even before the American Revolution.

Despite the proclamation of England's King George III in 1763 forbidding settlers to go into Indian territory west of the Appalachians, they did anyway. Conflict with the Indians, who believed the land to be theirs by right of occupation for thousands of years, became a natural consequence of this migration westward. But this was not a new problem; the encroachment on Indian lands had started with the first Europeans arriving on America's shores.

Dolley Madison, wife of President James Madison, was the second cousin of Walter Coles of Pittsylvania County, Virginia. *Library of Congress.*

Pittsylvania County families who migrated westward became part of that larger issue affecting the War of 1812. This author's fifth-great-grandfather Abraham Aaron migrated to Pittsylvania County in 1771, and after the Revolution, two of his sons migrated to Tennessee and Kentucky. That pattern occurred with other county families as well.

Because the invasion of settlers stressed Indian hunting grounds, undesirable contact with the Indians was unavoidable; consequently, treaties were made to pacify the situation. In 1771, John Donelson of Pittsylvania County, a member of the House of Burgesses in Virginia, was chosen by the governor to survey the boundary of lands that the Indians gave up above the Ohio River through the Treaty of Lochaber. Then, in 1772, Donelson met with Indian chiefs at Long Island on the Holston River to get boundary agreements.

However, despite treaties, hostilities persisted. Lord Dunmore, Virginia's governor, ordered General Andrew Lewis to mount an attack on Indian towns along the Ohio River. Several Pittsylvania County militia companies assisted Lewis's forces, which defeated the Indians on October 10, 1774, at what is now Point Pleasant, West Virginia. Later, during the American Revolution, Indian atrocities prompted two Pittsylvania County militia companies to be ordered beyond the Blue Ridge to the Holston River to quell Indian uprisings.

In 1779, John Donelson of Pittsylvania County and his family led a large contingent of settlers to Tennessee, and he, along with James Robertson, an explorer and associate of Daniel Boone, established Nashville. Conflicts with Indians accompanied Donelson's journey, and frequent attacks against the settlers continued along the frontier.

After the American Revolution, the 1783 Treaty of Paris, without any input or consideration of Native Americans, granted the lands east of the Mississippi to the United States, including what became known as the Northwest

John Donelson of Pittsylvania County, and a founder of Tennessee, surveyed Indian lands and negotiated with various tribes beyond the Appalachian Mountains during the 1770s. *Author's collection.*

Territory. This motivated more settlement, so by 1800, nearly 400,000 Americans lived west of the Appalachians and outnumbered the Indians. In the South, in areas claimed by Spain, the Creeks, Choctaws and Cherokees warred against the settlers moving into those areas, just as Indians above the Ohio River were doing.

By 1803, President Jefferson had purchased the Louisiana Territory, doubling the size of the United States. This act gave legitimacy to acquiring Indian lands by whatever means necessary, further provoking tensions on the frontier in the West.

In 1809, William Henry Harrison, governor of Indiana Territory, negotiated a treaty with various tribes for 3 million acres in Indiana and Illinois. The next year, an Indian chief named Tecumseh met with Harrison and claimed that the treaty was illegal. A war on white settlers resulted in an Indian defeat at the Battle of Tippecanoe River in 1811. Tecumseh then allied his forces with the British, and this Indian alliance would be a major factor along the Canadian border in the War of 1812.

After the war, the Indian "problem" would be solved, but not in favor of the Indians. Tecumseh had argued, "These lands are ours, and no one has the right to remove us. Because we were the first land owners; the Great Spirit above has appointed this place for us on which to light fires, and here we will remain." But it was not to be.

Pittsylvania County's support for Jefferson's direction for this country thus increased the possibilities of larger access to fertile and abundant lands beyond the horizon—lands where agriculture would thrive and new states would form, but lands cherished by American Indians as well.

In time, new states were also organized on lands once claimed by the Indians. Pittsylvania County, along with the rest of Virginia and the other southern states, gained political leverage in Congress as they collaborated with the new western states of Tennessee, Kentucky and Ohio. It was this numerically powerful voting bloc that overruled Federalist opposition and took the nation down the path toward the second war for independence.

Sectional differences between the commercial North and the agricultural South and the party politics of the Federalists and the Republicans, coupled with the conflicts with the Indians, were not the essential causes of the War of 1812, but they affected it significantly. These were internal issues that resulted from being a young country on the move, somewhat unsure of what it was to become. But there was more unfinished business with Great Britain that had been simmering since the writing of the Declaration of Independence.

Thomas Jefferson had listed in the Declaration of Independence causes for separation from Britain, and among them were some problems that were still not settled in 1812:

> *He* [George III] *has constrained our fellow Citizens taken Captive on the high Seas to bear Arms against their Country, to become the executioners of their friends and Brethren, or to fall themselves by their Hands.*

> *He has excited domestic insurrections amongst us, and has endeavored to bring on the inhabitants of our frontiers, the merciless Indian Savages, whose known rule of warfare, is an undistinguished destruction of all ages, sexes and conditions.*

As the War of 1812 approached, interference with American ships on the high seas—by France as well but mostly by Great Britain—resulted in the harassment of our coastal shipping and impressment of American sailors, forcing them to serve in the British navy. These issues were widely held up as the main causes of the War of 1812.

And even though by the start of the War of 1812 the British had finally abandoned their forts around the Great Lakes, as prescribed by the Treaty of Paris, which ended the American Revolutionary War, they were still active there. The March 7, 1812 edition of the *Niles' Weekly Register* printed the following: "We have but one opinion as to the cause of the depredations of the Indians, which was, and is, that they are instigated and supported by the British in Canada."

The constant violations by Great Britain of America's maritime rights and the British aiding and abetting the Indians in their vexation of settlers were the major issues that precipitated the War of 1812. It was an external war with Great Britain and, internally, a war between different sections of the country and their differing political views. In the end, the war would settle everything and nothing. But before all that happened, the country would engage in decades of disputes that would stir the pot of dissension. And when all was said and done, it seemed to some that war was the only solution.

Chapter 2

THE POWDER KEG

The approaching storm of war…if we cannot avert it, let us be prepared to meet it, supported by the…righteousness of our cause, and animated by the spirit of freemen.
—*Virginia governor W.H. Cabell, 1807*

Although events propelling America into the War of 1812 influenced Pittsylvania County indirectly, there was little that its citizens could do about them. Either way, eventually the county's militia and those from the county who joined the U.S. Army would find themselves in the midst of the fight.

George Washington's first administration was confronted with the French Revolution, which turned into anarchy and led to the execution of King Louis XVI. That revolution took wings and spread beyond the borders of France, putting other monarchies in jeopardy. Great Britain gathered a coalition to confront the French menace, meaning that after the American Revolution, France and Britain were at war again in 1793.

France desired America to honor the alliance of 1778 whereby the United States would defend French possessions against the British, specifically the French West Indies. But in 1793, George Washington declared neutrality, refusing to take sides in another European war.

Washington's decision not to support the French caused serious conflict in America. Thomas Jefferson believed that even with its excesses, the French Revolution was a victory for self-government. Even so, however much our country decided not to support France, Britain nonetheless began seizing hundreds of U.S. ships trading with the French West Indies and also resumed impressment, the kidnapping of American sailors to serve on British ships.

Protests from the American government over British actions got nowhere, and the confiscation of merchant ships and impressment of sailors continued. These issues were tolerated because both Britain and France, being at war with each other, needed American shipping. With the major shipping industry centered in New England, the profits from trading with both countries, according to some, far and again outweighed the loss of a few sailors and ships.

At that time, America had developed probably the largest merchant fleet in the world, trading with not only Britain and France via the West Indies but also other European countries. America's trading empire extended from China to Africa and South America.

With our 1778 treaty with France no longer binding and with Britain enjoying a favorable trading status with America, U.S. president John Adams, who followed Washington, encountered a further problem. French privateers began seizing American vessels trading with Britain. This interference in neutral trade, called the Quasi War, lasted from 1798 to 1800. However, Adams, without succumbing to pressure, refused to declare war against France, which again would have involved the United States in the ongoing European conflict.

As the war between England and France continued during the Jefferson administration, the Royal Navy gained control of the seas, while Napoleon, now in control of France, gained control of countries in Europe. He then instituted the Continental system, coercing countries in Europe to close the continent to British trade. This attempt by Napoleon to apply economic pressure on England resulted in a series of edicts and decrees from France and, in Britain, Orders in Council, all of which alternately closed British and French ports to American trade. The British motivation was to keep needed supplies away from Napoleon, while Napoleon's goal was to blockade England from American trade.

The attempt by Britain and France to stop neutral vessels from trading with the other created serious economic crises in the United States. Neutral vessels obeying the dictates of one violated those of the other. For instance, if American vessels sailed to European continental ports, they risked being captured by British ships since they violated the British blockade of Europe.

British Orders in Council demanded that goods being shipped to Europe had to either be in British vessels or that those neutral vessels had to stop at a

British port first. But if American ships stopped at British ports beforehand or after visiting European ports, they risked being captured by France. Thus, neutral shipping primarily by the United States, which had not taken sides in the war, was caught in a web of conflict not of its own making.

In 1805, a British fleet under Admiral Lord Nelson soundly defeated a combined French and Spanish squadron in the Battle of Trafalgar. After that, Britain ruled the seas, thus becoming the main culprit in the attack of American merchant shipping and impressment of its sailors. Britain held that its sailors were always British citizens, despite the fact that they often deserted and joined American ships. So the British navy believed that it had the right to stop U.S. merchant ships off America's shores or on the high seas if it suspected "its" sailors were aboard, although many whom it took were American citizens.

The British navy of that day had a despicable reputation; it was a life of misery. Gregory Fremont-Barnes in *Nelson's Sailors* offered what was a popular description of a British sailor of that day: "A press-ganged wretch living off weevil-infested, rotting food, motivated only by prize money, compelled to endure years of boredom and back-breaking work, and facing constant hazards aboard a floating hell, his conduct carefully scrutinized by his officers and discipline maintained with the lash."

Impressment of American Seamen by the British Navy. Illustration by Howard Pyle, 1884, Library of Congress.

Whether wholly true or not, many British sailors had been taken off the streets against their will, separated from families and children to be forced to serve on British ships. Thus, British sailors deserted with relative frequency to the American merchant marines or American navy, where pay and shipboard conditions were better. The United States Navy was a world apart from the brutal life aboard ships of Britain's navy and merchant fleet. Page Smith, in *The Shaping of America*, noted that British sailors so routinely deserted British ships to the extent that the British had to "lay up ships for lack of crews to man them." In fact, at Norfolk, Virginia, "the entire crew of a British vessel signed on to an American warship."

But it wasn't just the fact that Britain wanted "its" own sailors back; the British also took whomever they cared to off American ships, without much concern about whether or not they were former British citizens. It is estimated that between 1796 and 1801, about two thousand American sailors were impressed. Over time, estimates ranged up to six thousand Americans taken by the British navy. Merchant ships especially were confiscated and sold, and their crews were imprisoned.

It was this arrogant and contemptuous attitude on the part of the British toward America that showed a lack of respect for America's sovereignty. The United States had tried time and again to confront the British with this unlawful behavior, but to no avail.

Ultimately, the issues of "free trade and sailors' rights" became the cry of a war for which the country was woefully unprepared. National honor was being besmirched by an overreaching mother country, which acted as if its former colonies were powerless to do anything but complain. The British would not recognize America's neutrality, and when they stopped American ships on the high seas, boarded them and took whomever they decided was British, they disregarded any notion that invading our ships was invading our nation.

Therefore, it can be argued that Great Britain declared war on America first. Great Britain knew that America needed its trade regardless, and due to America's military weakness, Britain ignored our pleas to stop its violations of our sovereignty. It was an empire with colonies around the world; the United States was struggling with the concept of what it meant to be a nation united while at the same time struggling for a place in the international arena. But worse was yet to come before the dogs of war were released.

It happened on June 22, 1807. The USS *Chesapeake*, a thirty-eight-gun frigate under the command of Commodore James Barron, headed out to sea from the Hampton Roads port of Norfolk, Virginia, destined for the Mediterranean Sea. The *Chesapeake* would later be captured in a battle off Boston with the HMS *Shannon* six years later, but not this time. This time, the HMS *Leopard*, a fifty-gun man-of-war, had other intentions.

Captain Salisbury Humphreys of the *Leopard* pulled his ship alongside the *Chesapeake* and asked that a British party be allowed to board the *Chesapeake* to deliver a message sent to Humphreys from Admiral Berkeley, commander of the British Atlantic station at Halifax, Nova Scotia.

The message from Berkeley to all ship captains in the area of the bay instructed them to stop the *Chesapeake* and demand the return of four particular seaman or else use force if necessary. Commodore Barron refused to comply and sent the British party back to the *Leopard*. As soon as Humphreys read Barron's response, his ship opened fire on the *Chesapeake* with six broadsides at close range, killing three American sailors; wounding eighteen others, including Commodore Barron; and severely damaging the ship.

Being unprepared for battle, as a British attack of that sort was unexpected, Barron surrendered the *Chesapeake*. A British boarding party came onto the American vessel, mustered the men on deck and forcibly took the four seamen in question. As it eventually came to be known, three of them were American citizens who had been impressed by the British previously.

Only one of those was a deserter from the British navy, who, unbeknownst to Commodore Barron, had changed his name when he enlisted on the *Chesapeake*. The other three were eventually released, but the former deserter was hanged in Halifax from the yardarm of the *Leopard*.

When the *Chesapeake* returned to Norfolk and the news leaked out, it spread rapidly. The British had not just attacked and impressed seamen from a merchant ship; they had, for the first time, attacked a U.S. Navy warship. Public meetings across the nation condemned the British. For many Americans, the attack on one of the country's navy ships and the unwarranted killing of U.S. citizens was the final provocation in a long series of such actions, and most believed that war was imminent.

The next day, the *Norfolk Ledger* published the story of the attack and concluded, "There can be but one sentiment in the heart of every American. The independence of our country has been attacked, and in defending it our fellow citizens have been killed.... Every national ship is considered as a part of the nation's territory."

On the evening of the twenty-fourth, a meeting of citizens of Norfolk and Portsmouth, chaired by Brigadier General Thomas Matthews of the

The USS *Chesapeake* was attacked on June 22, 1807, by the British warship HMS *Leopard*, which impressed four sailors from the American frigate. *Illustration by Fred S. Cozzens, 1897, Library of Congress.*

Virginia Militia, passed a resolution breaking off communication with British ships, forbidding them in any way to receive supplies or provisions or allowing their agents, in this case the British consul in Norfolk, to contact those ships or their crew.

The Norfolk mayor contacted the commandant of militia to "hold in readiness an armed force for the purposes of defense." The resolution spoke of those killed on the *Chesapeake* as "victims of British and premeditated assassination." That appeared to be pretty much the reaction of the rest of the country. On July 2, President Thomas Jefferson issued a proclamation ordering all British ships out of American waters and refused to allow British vessels into American ports or harbors.

On July 3, Commodore Douglas on the HMS *Bellona*, angered by the prohibition of British ships in Lynnhaven Bay being unable to communicate with the British consul in Norfolk, wrote, "I am therefore determined, if this infringement is not immediately annulled, to prohibit every vessel bound in or out of Norfolk to proceed to their destination." Further, he threatened, "you must also be aware that it has been, and still is, in my power to obstruct the whole trade of the Chesapeake."

By July 6, with the standoff continuing, Secretary of War Henry Dearborn had authorized the governor of Virginia, William H. Cabell, and those of "the several states" as well, to bring their state militias to readiness for action. Virginia's quota of the 100,000 authorized to be federalized by Congress in April 1806 for national emergencies was 11,563. Each county, including Pittsylvania, would have been expected to mobilize its respective companies at the adjutant general's order.

The governor would have likely contacted Pittsylvania's 42nd Regiment under Lieutenant Colonel Daniel Coleman and the 101st Regiment under Lieutenant Colonel Thomas Wooding. Both men also served in the Virginia legislature representing Pittsylvania County during this time. Although the Pittsylvania Militia was not called up, there is little doubt that it was alerted to the situation and took stock of its own preparedness.

In Richmond, an inventory of arms and munitions needed for militia was taken at the Manufactory of Arms, a state-owned facility established to provide militia with firearms and related accoutrements. Due diligence was also paid to repairs needed at Fort Norfolk, including cannons mounted around the battlements.

On December 8, 1807, Virginia's governor, W.H. Cabell, addressed the opening session of the House of Delegates in Richmond, informing the body of the circumstances related to the *Chesapeake*. In attendance would have been Thomas Wooding and Rawley White from Pittsylvania, and they would have heard the governor remark, "The capes of Virginia have been made the theater of outrage unprecedented in the history of nations." The governor went on to say that the British, in defiance of the president's proclamation, remained within the capes until October, although they did not carry out any attack along Virginia's shores.

He further warned the body that Congress was then considering a law to suspend almost all commercial intercourse with Britain and cautioned of "the clouds now collecting on our horizon, indicating the approaching storm of war…But if we cannot avert it, let us be prepared to meet it, supported by the conscious righteousness of our cause, and animated by the spirit of freemen."

Although the nation anticipated war, Jefferson encouraged Congress to respond to Britain's actions (and, to a lesser extent, France's) with commercial rather than military warfare. So, on December 22, Jefferson signed into law the Embargo Act of 1807. That, too, would cause an outrage, to a greater extent in America than in Britain. The maritime issues that pushed the embargo did not directly involve Pittsylvania County but affected it economically, leaving it with no method to export tobacco and other agricultural commodities or import British goods.

Chapter 3

DAMBARGO

Our country! In her intercourse with foreign nations may she be always in the
right, but our country, right or wrong.
—U.S. Navy captain Stephen Decatur, 1816

The Embargo Act of 1807 was the most serious effort thus far to stop British interference with American shipping and the impressment of American sailors. Previously, Jefferson's administration had already initiated the Non-Importation Act of 1806, which forbade importing certain goods from Great Britain—clothing, for example. This was suspended for some time with the hopes that negotiations with Britain would be successful.

When it was replaced by the Embargo Act, not only importing but also the exporting of any goods whatsoever to Great Britain was forbidden. Actually, trade was cut off to all countries. Ships were not to leave their harbors unless involved in coastal trade. Up and down the East Coast of the United States, ships were idled, and seamen were put on the streets.

The embargo was supposed to cause such commercial anguish to both Britain and France that they would be forced to renounce their belligerent attitudes toward the United States and repeal their restrictive orders and decrees that made our nation's trade with either one nearly impossible. In the *War and Society Journal* article "The Making of the Chesapeake-Leopard Affair," Joshua Wolf brings to the forefront the thinking of the time. The nation's question became "[h]ow much of the liberty gained in the Revolution was being sacrificed through the nation's inaction? Impressment was an issue that excited passions. Politicians, newspaper editors, merchants, seamen, ship captains, and balladeers all recognized impressment was a crime perpetrated against United States citizens."

This debate, of course, had been going on before the *Chesapeake-Leopard* affair, but it skyrocketed afterward. Something had to be done. The nation was being humiliated, but what Jefferson did only made things worse within the country, while not having the effect he thought it would on Britain and France.

Statistics for the years between 1804 and 1806 indicate that the United States was by far the major exporter of flour, corn, timber and other wood products compared to Great Britain; Ireland; the British Provinces, including British West Indies and Canada; and other countries combined. Thus, any disruption in exports of these agricultural products would certainly affect agricultural regions in the United States.

As a Founding Father of America, Jefferson knew that the nonimportation acts before the Revolution had caused England to reverse its coercive tax acts against the colonies, until finally a small tax on tea continued, which helped set off the Revolutionary War. This time, though, that strategy didn't work, for England found other sources of materials and markets for its goods.

Additionally, New England shippers, who were the most affected by it, evaded the act in a wholesale manner. Outright evasion and loopholes in the law prevented the law from being universally enforced. As a result, from 1807 to 1812, it is estimated that Britain, France and their allies seized at least nine hundred American ships, cargoes and crews.

Losing a ship's cargo and a seaman from impressment was no small matter, but the biggest effect was on the American economy. Exports dropped from $108 million in 1807 to $22 million in 1808. Thus, the embargo brought economic depression not experienced since the resistance by American colonies in the previous century.

Shipping interests in New England suffered, but agriculture in the South and West was also affected. Outlets for grain, cotton and tobacco and other southern agricultural products were closed off, and the prices for those commodities were severely affected. In the *American Embargo, 1807–1809*, Walter Jennings pointed out that "[t]he prices of agricultural products went up, imported articles went up, land and slaves depreciated in value, mortgages were foreclosed…speculators thrived by buying up products at low prices, and money lenders obtained exorbitant interest."

Jennings concluded, "The true burden of the embargo fell on the Southern States, but most severely on the great state of Virginia…. Tobacco, wheat, flour and corn of Virginia sought in vain for a market." To which he added, "Tobacco was worthless." Tobacco, most of which came from Virginia and Maryland, experienced extreme decline, with prices falling about 85 percent from 1807 to 1808.

Since tobacco was a primary crop for Pittsylvania County, the embargo would have seriously reduced exports of the golden leaf and, in return, reduced imports so desired by plantations. Like other Virginia citizens, Pittsylvania farmers would have also used the profit from the present year's tobacco crop to pay year-old debts and buy necessities for the next year. So, not being able to export tobacco and import goods would have brought economic woe in various distressing ways to the county. As Jennings reasoned, "With his products well-nigh unsalable and his credit poor, the farmer certainly had a hard row to hoe." It was said that the embargo was "like cutting one's throat to cure the nosebleed."

Of course, the greatest hue and cry was raised mostly by the maritime regions of New York and New England, even while the New England areas continued to profit from smuggling. Identified mostly as Federalist strongholds, these areas played up the damage to American commerce. Jefferson was vilified in the press and the halls of Congress, mostly by Federalists and their sympathizers.

In his effort to avoid war, Jefferson had pressed Congress to pass the Embargo Act but had let loose the dogs of war within American borders and divided the country. Its critics called it the "Dambargo" or "O Grab Me" (*embargo* spelled backward), the latter depicted by a cartoon showing a turtle snapping at the American economy.

The act was so unpopular in Federalist-dominated areas of New England that it was referred to as a "monster" and a "poisonous dragon." On December 22, 1808, the first anniversary of the embargo, New England towns expressed their mourning dramatically. Ships flew flags at half-mast, their crews marched in the street to dismal music and church bells tolled.

Opposition referred to the embargo as a "decree of slavery," and newspapers spewed forth incendiary language that appeared to prompt open rebellion. A few others were instruments of caution. On January 28, 1809, a Danville, Vermont newspaper, the *North Star*, headlined one edition with "Seeds of Insurrection," commenting on the "serious fears of rebellion against the laws of our country" and enjoining, "Let us pause, and consider the calamities of civil war."

The attitude in New England was not universal across America, as expressed by a letter on January 18, 1809, from the U.S. secretary of war

Cartoon with merchants evading "O Grab Me" (*embargo* spelled backward). Refers to the extreme dissatisfaction by American merchants over the 1807 embargo enacted by the Jefferson administration. *Wikimedia.org.*

to the Virginia governor. The secretary of war noted, "The pressure of the Embargo, although sensibly felt by every description of our Fellow-Citizens, has yet been cheerfully borne by most of them under a conviction that it was a temporary evil, and a necessary one to save us from greater and more permanent evils—the loss of property and surrender of rights."

The secretary then referred to the unprincipled men on the seacoast and frontiers who were "fraudulently evading it" and the need to put an end to this "scandalous insubordination to the laws." Citizens of Pittsylvania County, although seriously affected by the economic downturn due to the embargo, were solid supporters of Jefferson and must have borne the effects with fortitude. Even Patrick County, next door to Pittsylvania, passed a resolution:

We pledge ourselves that at the hazard of our lives and fortunes we will support the honor and dignity of our country and prove ourselves worthy of the glorious heritage derived to us by the blood and treasure of our fathers, and cheerfully submit to all the privations incident to a state of war without murmur.

There can be little doubt that Pittsylvania citizens felt the same. Even so, by March 1, 1809, the unpopularity of the act had caused it to be repealed right before Jefferson's second term was over. However, one good result did come from the embargo. With imports cut off, people sought to develop their own industry. In 1808, in Richmond, Governor William H. Cabell urged all Virginians to adopt a "system of domestic manufactures as would render them independent of foreign nations."

In the first survey of manufacturing and domestic products in 1810, as described in *A Statement of the Arts and Manufactures of the United States of America*, Pittsylvania County had, among other industries, two hat factories and five tanneries, where hides were made into 113,428 shoes, boots, slippers and saddles. The county also produced 750 pounds of gunpowder. The county's cotton crop produced 179,606 yards of cotton goods from 996 family looms.

Regardless of the upsurge in manufacturing and home industries, Federalists in 1808 passed a resolution in New York: "Resolved, That the embargo is an oppressive and ruinous measure operating with only destructive energy on ourselves, while it has rendered us objects of contempt and ridicule of that nation against which it was invidiously directed." And yet, despite Federalist opposition to the Republican policies, Pittsylvania County citizens, still suffering under the Embargo Act, strongly supported Jefferson's secretary of state, James Madison, for president.

Madison had Congress replace the embargo with the Non-Intercourse Act, which forbade trade with Britain and France and their colonies but opened up trade with other countries. If either Britain or France lifted its restrictive orders and decrees, then the Non-Intercourse Act would be lifted for that country. Once again, the act failed in its intended purpose.

Therefore, in May 1810, Congress passed Macon's Bill No. 2, which lifted trade restrictions with both Britain and France; however, if one repealed its trade restrictions against America, then America would reinstitute a trade embargo on the other. This feeble effort only further exacerbated the problem. Britain, for whom the act was mostly directed, would not yield on impressment or forcefully boarding American ships.

None of the negotiations, embargos or any other diplomatic efforts resolved the situation. With the newly elected Twelfth Congress, though, there was a major change in political orientation of the House of Representatives. With the embargo over and prosperity throughout the country renewed, the Federalist opposition lost seats in Congress, while confidence in the Democratic-Republican Party was restored. It regained a two-thirds majority in the House, with Pittsylvania County and the rest of

Virginia voting heavily Republican, electing seventeen Republicans and only five Federalists for its twenty-two seats.

The Twelfth Congress comprised seventy new congressmen all under forty years of age and represented a new breed of members from the South and West (Kentucky, Tennessee and Ohio), who were mostly Democratic-Republicans. Henry Clay of Kentucky was elected Speaker of the House of Representatives in his first term and became a stalwart advocate of war with Great Britain. He saw the impressment issue in stark reality, as noted by his speech before the House of Representatives in January 1813: "The naked truth is, she [Great Britain] comes, by her press-gangs, on board of our vessels, seizes our native seamen, as well as naturalized, and drags them into her service."

Like Clay, these newly elected "War Hawks," as they were unceremoniously dubbed, resented the attacks on national honor. They disregarded New England objections that losing a sailor once in a while was no cause for war and demanded that America's honor be defended and its sovereignty upheld. It is safe to say that as a stronghold of Democratic-Republican sentiment, Pittsylvania County applauded this view.

Meeting for the first time in November 4, 1811, the new Congress advocated military preparations in advance of likely war. Adding fuel to the argument was another event, one that created a firestorm and supported the War Hawks' insistence that war was necessary to resolve this impasse with England.

On May 16, 1811, the forty-four-gun U.S. frigate *President*, anchored in Chesapeake Bay, was told to seek out the British man-of-war *Guerriere*, which had recently forced a boarding party on the merchant ship *Spitfire* and impressed a native of Maine into British service. When the *President* saw what it thought was the *Guerriere* during the night, the ship, actually the British *Little Belt*, refused to identify itself; in the confusion of the darkness, the ships fired at each other. The *President* launched such a devastating cannonade that the *Little Belt* was rendered out of commission and sailed back to the British Naval Station at Halifax.

Although the *President*'s captain was remorseful over the mistaken identity, he was adamant that the British had fired first. Secretary of War James Monroe defended the *President*'s actions, noting that the United States had the right to investigate suspicious men-of-war near its shores. The British response was typified by an article in the *London Courier* that insisted that the United States had attacked the *Little Belt* first and without provocation: "The blood of our murdered countrymen must be avenged and WAR MUST ENSUE. We have behaved toward America with UNEXAMPLED FORBEARANCE, but the forbearance produced INSOLENCE, AND THAT INSOLENCE MUST BE PUNISHED."

The hypocrisy of such a statement, when the reverse was true, could only ignite America's passions against England. By the fall of 1811, although there was opposition in Congress and other parts of the nation, the War Hawks were demanding war with Great Britain. They would soon have their way. But like most wars, this one would not go as planned.

Chapter 4

THE WAR NO ONE WANTED

*If ever there was a just cause for war in the sight of almighty God
this cause is on our side.*
—*John Quincy Adams, 1812*

The year 1812 began in crisis, a dark foreshadowing of things to come. In January, the Great Comet of 1812 lit up the dark skies over America in its nearest approach to Earth, ironically forecasting in many minds the end of the world. Also, in January and February, the most powerful earthquakes ever recorded in the eastern United States centered in New Madrid, Missouri. The devastating series of shockwaves, starting back in December 1811, rang church bells in Boston; woke people from their sleep in Charleston, South Carolina; cracked sidewalks in Washington, D.C.; and caused the Mississippi River to run backward. Mount Tambora, ten thousand miles away in Indonesia, began spewing out dark clouds of ash in 1812 that culminated in 1815 in one of the most massive volcanic eruptions ever recorded. On June 24, Napoleon's Grand Armee, the largest European force ever assembled since the Crusades, began what would become its failed invasion of Russia.

But in Washington, D.C., in June 1812, Napoleon's war, volcanoes, comets and devastating earthquakes were the least of worries. Another battle had been brewing there, a different kind of battle, with its own brand of thunder and chaos destined to be unleashed. After a decade of mounting tension between the United States and Great Britain, the dark clouds of war hung low over the American nation.

In the winter and spring of 1812, inflamed passions in Congress and in newspapers throughout the nation for and against war fueled speculation about the outcome of the continuing conflict with Great Britain. In December 1811, Henry Clay had offered this compelling reason for war:

We are called upon to submit to debasement, dishonor and disgrace— to bow the neck to royal insolence…. What nation, what individual was ever taught, in the schools of ignominious submission, the patriotic lessons of freedom and independence?…It was not by submission that our fathers achieved independence. They saw a long train of oppressive measures terminating in that total annihilation of liberty and did not hesitate to resist them.

Edward Coles, in a letter written thirty-seven years later, on January 21, 1859, discussed the mounting pressure for war prevalent during that time. He said that President Madison believed that "the sword was not to be resorted to until the pen had done all it could do." However, "[w]hile negotiations were going on, a class of irritable men, to be found in all communities, were eager for war, and were fretful and impatient at delay." Coles further stated, "These were the hotspurs of the day, who censured all who were not as pugnacious as themselves." They thought that once war was declared and one drop of American blood was spilled, the ranks of the army would be filled with men and the treasury with money. Coles indicated that while President Madison refused to be impulsive on this issue, even he finally saw it as the only solution.

However, going to war would not be that easy. And yet in early 1812, Pittsylvania County would find itself in the midst of preparations for such a possibility. Opposition by most New England members did not deter Congress in January 1812 from authorizing that the U.S. Army be increased to 35,600. But despite all efforts to garner enlistments, by June 1812, total army strength amounted to less than one-third of that number.

In Virginia, tragedy had struck in December 1811 when the governor died in a theater fire in Richmond. Because of that circumstance, James Barbour became governor that January and immediately concerned himself with issues necessary to get the state prepared should war come. He published a proclamation standardizing uniforms to more easily identify officers and various types of units by their dress. Early on, Barbour was also concerned with the defense of Norfolk and the nearby Gosport Naval Yard, a support base for various U.S. Navy squadrons.

On March 21, 1812, despite continued attempts by America to resolve the crisis with Great Britain, their minister to the United States announced that Britain's Orders in Council, which concerned British interference in America's neutral shipping and the impressment of its sailors into their navy, would not be repealed. There seemed to be no turning back from armed conflict.

Andrew Jackson of Tennessee raised an important question as he argued for war with Great Britain. "Who are we?" he ventured. It was a core question that underscored what the coming war would ultimately be about: national identity. He answered with: "Sons of America: the citizens of the only republic now existing in the world; and the only people on earth who possess rights, liberties, and property which they dare call their own." Those were concepts that embodied America's sovereignty on the high seas as well as on land.

To avert the approaching crisis, a ninety-day embargo against Great Britain was initiated by President Madison on April 4, 1812. This cutoff of trade with Britain's merchants was a last-ditch effort to bring Great Britain to the negotiating table to resolve the issues.

On April 15, 1812, U.S. Secretary of War Eustis relayed a proclamation from President Madison for the governors of the states to "organize, arm, and equip [militia] and hold in readiness to march at a moment's warning their respective proportions." The president's quota was 100,000 men, with Virginia's allotment still being about 12,000.

In Pittsylvania County, as well as the rest of Virginia, all able-bodied white males between eighteen and forty-five were duty bound to take up arms as needed. The county's 42nd and 101st Regiments, which still enjoyed the leadership of Colonels Daniel Coleman and Thomas Wooding, would have been put on alert.

As the nation inched closer to conflict, Pittsylvania County court records suggest growing concern about the war. From February through June 1812, more than thirty captains, lieutenants and ensigns presented their commissions to the county court and had them approved after taking the required oath to support the Constitution of the United States. Some joined regular Virginia Militia infantry regiments, as well as light infantry units. Others became officers of cavalry, rifle or artillery companies.

As June approached, it appeared inevitable that a second war of independence would be fought. That moment in history was reflected in a letter dated May 12, 1812, from President Madison's wife, Dolley, to her sister, Anna Cutts: "My dear Sister, John Randolph has been firing away at the House this morning against the declaration of War, but we suppose it will have little effect."

According to Stuart Butler in a *Richmond-Times Dispatch* article, Randolph was a Republican but "did everything he could to obstruct all measures supporting the war. Like the Federalists, he considered the war foolish, ruinous of the public credit, a dangerous increase in presidential powers and likely to end in humiliation and defeat."

Dolley Madison appeared to pay Randolph's rantings little mind. Instead, she seemed more interested in the following reference in the letter: "Catherine Coles' son Walter [their second cousin], he is here now and made a Lieutenant in the Army—he looks just as he did when you and I staid [*sic*] with him in Chestnut St."

Coles's enlistment in the army was indicative of the war fever that had been spreading throughout Virginia prior to that June and was no doubt related to Congress's call for army recruits. *A List of Officers in the Army of the United States 1779 to 1900* notes that Walter Coles and Samuel Hairston Jr. of Pittsylvania County both enlisted on March 12, 1812. By July 6, 1812, Coles was listed as a second lieutenant in the 2nd Light Dragoons (Cavalry), and Hairston was a second lieutenant in the U.S. Army 20th Infantry. Both men's regiments were sent north toward Canada.

After the war, Coles would build the present-day Coles Hill, a few miles from Chalk Level, on land inherited from his father, Isaac Coles, who had served in the first U.S. Congress. Hairston, who would later build the Oak Hill plantation in Pittsylvania County, would become one of the richest men and one of the largest slave owners in the South after the war.

As war tension mounted, the British realized that if Napoleon's legions advancing on Russia were successful, their global empire would be in jeopardy. A war with America and France at the same time would only favor France, since Britain would be fighting a war on two fronts. Further, Britain was experiencing a poor grain crop that year, and provisions for its troops in the European theater necessitated continued peace with America.

Although no widespread support for the war existed in the United States, the drums of war continued to beat loudest with the War Hawks in Congress. The end game began on June 1, 1812, when Edward Coles, personal secretary of President Madison and another cousin of Walter Coles, walked into the House of Representatives at the Capitol and laid a message from the president on the Speaker's desk. The House was cleared of all except members, and the message was read and debated.

Military commission of Samuel Hairston of Pittsylvania County, dated July 23, 1812, and signed by President James Madison, appointing him second lieutenant in the U.S. Army 20th Infantry Regiment. *Melissa Sims Hairston and Robert Sims.*

In his message to Congress, the president discussed the history of America's efforts to reconcile its differences with Britain and emphasized the grievances that the United States had against the mother country. The impressment of sailors topped the list of issues in Madison's message. He wrote:

47

British cruisers have been in the continued practice of violating the American flag on the great highway of nations, and of seizing and carrying off persons sailing under it…thousands of American citizens have been torn from their country and from everything dear to them; have been dragged on board ships of war of a foreign nation and exposed, under the severities of their discipline, to be exiled to the most distant and deadly climes, to risk their lives in the battles of their oppressors, and to be the melancholy instruments of taking away those of their own brethren.

British cruisers have been in the practice also of violating the rights and the peace of our coasts. They hover over and harass our entering and departing commerce [and] *have wantonly spilt American blood within the sanctuary of our territorial jurisdiction.*

Our commerce has been plundered in every sea, the great staples of our country have been cut off from their legitimate markets, and a destructive blow aimed at our agricultural and maritime interests.

Madison also noted the savage attacks by Indians on settlers on the frontier and concluded that it occurred "among tribes in constant intercourse with British traders and garrisons."

By June 4, the House had voted seventy-nine to forty-nine in favor of war with Great Britain. During the next two weeks, the Senate heatedly debated

James Madison, fourth president of the United States (1809–1817). *Wikimedia Commons.*

the issues and finally voted nineteen to thirteen for war, as well against the mother country. Besides being the first time that the United States had declared war on a foreign nation, this still remains the closest war vote in American history. It also revealed the deep divisions in the country; none of the thirty-nine Federalists in Congress voted for it, referring to it sarcastically as "Mr. Madison's War."

On June 18, President Madison signed the declaration of war, unaware that two days earlier, the British had "revoked" the dreaded Orders in Council. However, the revocation only affected the stopping of ships on the high seas, not impressment. Even so, the British revocation of the Orders was conditional, requiring the United States to open its ports once again to British ships, while conveniently forgetting that for years American ports were open while the country gave Britain chance after chance to stop impressment and the piracy of our merchant ships on the open sea.

Britain, in its June 1812 decree, also insisted that "nothing...shall... preclude His Royal Highness the Prince Regent, if circumstances shall so require, from restoring...the orders...or from taking such other measures of retaliation...as may appear to His Royal Highness to be just and necessary." In other words, the British did not acknowledge our sovereignty on the seas but just tried to avoid war.

With war declared against them, the British were angry beyond description. Instead of accepting responsibility for their actions, they made excuses. In his *History of the Late War*, published in 1832, David Thompson of Scotland, who served with Canadian forces during the War of 1812, relegated the decision of the United States to declare War in 1812 as the result of "a spirit of prejudice, distrust and rancor against Great Britain, in the minds of Americans." He believed that this war resulted solely from the angry separation of the Thirteen Colonies from the mother country in 1776. And that prior prejudice against the mother country made it impossible for Americans to judge the actions of Britain impartially regarding the issues related to the War of 1812.

Canadian author Gilbert Auchinleck, in his highly biased *History of the War Between Great Britain and the United States of America*, published in Toronto in 1855, ruled that the American government had been "thirsting for strife with Great Britain" and that Jefferson and Madison had been sympathizers with France against Britain. Furthermore, he questioned the declaration of war:

> *How could it enter into their minds...that the interests of the United States would be best promoted by selecting for their adversary the one of the two offending nations which, in peace maintained with them the closest relations, founded on commerce eminently prosperous and profitable; and, in war, had the means of giving them the heaviest blows.*

But the declaration of war was about more than economics. Tony Horowitz, in the June 2012 *Smithsonian Magazine*, pointed out the dilemma that the United States faced in 1812: "The U.S. had the excuse of being very young and insecure. The Constitution wasn't yet 25 years old, the nation remained a shaky experiment, and Britain still behaved in a neo-colonial fashion." The country was at a crossroads, and something had to be done.

With war against Britain now official, Virginia's Governor Barbour issued a broadside from Richmond on June 25, to be distributed to majors and captains of regiments. One can only imagine the patriotic response when news of war and the governor's message reached Pittsylvania County militiamen. Governor Barbour noted, "The long anticipated event has at length occurred: America has closed with Great Britain in a solemn appeal to the God of Battles, and looks to the energy of her Citizens for that redress of her wrongs which she has demanded of her enemies in vain…. It is a period that will decide the character and fate of America." He indicated, too, that it would require "an ardent devotion to her cause, a determination to encounter every…danger which the conflict may produce."

As the nation entered further into the summer of 1812, even more men had their commissions as officers in the Pittsylvania County militia approved and forwarded to the governor for his certification. The county of Pittsylvania was ready to defend Virginia.

And the citizens of Pittsylvania County would no doubt have heeded the appeal to patriotism that Governor Barbour raised in Richmond that September in an effort to solicit funds from counties for the "accommodation and comfort of drafts, volunteers or their families." Primarily, it was an effort to supply the needs of Virginia troops headed to the Northwest Territory in that campaign against the British and Indians. Barbour wrote:

> Our country, after manifesting a love of peace unexampled in the annals of the world, has been compelled to the sword. The enemy has allied itself with our savage neighbors. Already the tomahawk and scalping knife are reeking with the blood of women and children on the frontier and the trees of the wilderness gleam with the blaze of their humble dwellings. Numbers of our citizens, in obedience to the call of their country, resolved to avenge her wrongs and maintain her rights, have left their homes, and those objects of love who made home delightful. And put on the habiliments of war.

While it is not recorded that any Pittsylvania County soldiers accompanied that journey northward, it is hard to imagine Barbour's words not resonating with county citizens since there was, to a large degree, unity of mind and spirit about the necessity of this war throughout the state. Regardless of where the battle was, Pittsylvania County's citizens had a stake in the outcome as much as all other countrymen.

First page of a letter by Philip Grasty of Pittsylvania County to
Virginia governor James Barbour, dated May 20, 1812, concerning the
commission of officers for the Virginia militia, followed by a patriotic
statement. *Executive Letters Received, Record Group 3, Library of Virginia,
Stuart Butler.*

With war declared, patriotism found a willing audience. If this letter from Philip L. Grasty of Pittsylvania County to Governor Barbour, dated May 20, 1812, is any indication, citizens of Pittsylvania were fully supportive of defending the honor and independence of this country. Grasty wrote:

> *The present crisis presents to the mind features similar to the last revolution—a period which calls a loud for love of country, for pure patriotism—no one sir ought to look on our situation with indifference—possessed of liberty (dearly bought) with all its choicest blessings. None but a traitor to his country would sacrifice her on the altar of Emperors or Kings—& I anticipate with pleasure the mutual defence [sic] which will be made of the rights & liberties of our country.*

No doubt Virginians everywhere would have agreed.

Chapter 5

OH! CANADA

Strike whenever we can reach the enemy, at sea and on land. But if we fail, let us fail like men…and expire together in one common struggle.
—Henry Clay, Speaker, House of Representatives, 1812

C anada was the prime target in our dispute with Britain over free trade and sailors' rights in the War of 1812. Neither of these was a particular issue between the United States and Canada, but Canada seemed vulnerable and the only place where the United States could prosecute the war against the British empire. And it looked tantalizingly simple to do. An essay on the Discriminating General, a Canadian website, lists the negatives for Canada: "The British Provinces lacked the population, the food supplies, the military equipment, the manufacturing resources and the troops available to the United States."

According to the *Army Historical Series*, when the War of 1812 began, the United States' population amounted to 7.7 million people. Along the Canadian border, small detachments of American Regular Army personnel manned a series of forts: Fort Mackinac, between Lake Michigan and Lake Heron; Fort Dearborn, at present-day Chicago; Fort Detroit; and Fort Niagara, near the entrance of the Niagara River into Lake Erie.

Canada had a population of only 500,000, with a total of 7,000 British and Canadian regulars and a reservoir of 10,000 militiamen from which to draw, compared to the 450,000 militia in the United States. Also, Britain had most of its troops and most of its thousand or so ships fighting

Napoleon in Europe. The most powerful navy in the world could spare only forty-five warships and as many smaller vessels to engage America. And those were deployed in a variety of missions—namely, to escort British merchant ships, protect the St. Lawrence River, blockade American ports and engage the small American navy, which consisted of six frigates and fourteen other vessels.

All things considered, the mission to invade Canada seemed very lopsided in favor of the United States, not to mention that many people in Canada were recent emigrants from the United States and likely would not think of taking up arms against their former country. Canadians were somewhat demoralized, too, knowing that the overwhelming superiority of American forces would make resistance useless. Of course, most of the Indians had aligned themselves with the British, providing the British with an extra weapon that the United States did not share.

Still, it was almost unthinkable that America could not successfully invade Canada and stop the British menace at its border. As Richard Buel noted in *America on the Brink*, "The notion that a nation of seven million souls was powerless to defend itself against a European adversary seemed preposterous."

Therefore, an invasion of Canada was thought to bring the most results and quickest victories. Defeating Canada would quell the British-inspired Indian uprisings ongoing in the northwestern territories and would cut off naval stores and timber that Britain depended on for its ships. What better way to get Great Britain to see the error of its ways and come to the bargaining table.

Of course, British writers chose to see the invasion of Canada in a different light. For instance, Winston Churchill, in his *History of the English Speaking People*, wrote that impressment was not the real issue but rather the "lust for land," meaning that the war was about annexing Canada. But that comment ignores the obvious, as presented by George Tindall in *America: Narrative History of America*: "The only place where the United States could effectively strike at the British was Canada."

So, without a doubt, the takeover of Canada seemed like a sure thing. Thomas Jefferson said that it was a "matter of mere marching." Henry Clay of Kentucky, the Speaker of the House of Representatives, boasted in a speech to Congress in 1812, "I verily believe that the militia of Kentucky are alone competent to place Montreal and Upper Canada at your feet." John Calhoun of South Carolina, also one of the newly elected War Hawks, offered this prediction: "I believe in four weeks from the time a declaration is heard on our frontier, the whole of Upper Canada and a part of Lower Canada will be in our power."

But taking Canada was not without its problems. There was plenty of opposition from the Federalists at home. Richard Buel reasoned in *America on the Brink* that "[m]ost Federalists in Congress did all they could to deny the government resources it needed to invade Canada and bring the war to a successful conclusion. New England towns refused to pay federal taxes, and Massachusetts, Connecticut and Rhode Island along with New Hampshire and Vermont discouraged enlistments and refused to allow the U.S. government access to their militia."

This struggle between the Federalist Party and the Republican-controlled governments of Jefferson and, later, Madison was in itself a major threat to the nation, even in some respects more than Great Britain and France. While not allowing their militias to participate in the invasion of Canada, these Federalist states engaged in smuggling and illegal trade along the Canadian border.

The population of Canada was confined to two provinces. Upper Canada, with its southern border stretched along the Great Lakes, was the precursor of today's Ontario. Lower Canada, the forerunner of the modern-day Quebec province, encompassed Montreal, Quebec City and the St. Lawrence River area. The northeastern part of Lower Canada bordered the Atlantic Ocean and the territories of New Brunswick, Nova Scotia and Newfoundland.

Instead of concentrating all its forces at one point of attack, the United States' war planners advised a three-pronged attack on Canada, none of which was successful. There would be an attack on Montreal for control of the St. Lawrence River: one into the Niagara River frontier and one at Detroit, on the westernmost end of Lake Erie. At the same time, a second theater of war emerged on the high seas, as America, with its small navy and privateers, took the offensive against British commerce.

The war in the Northwest began on a disheartening note in July 1812 with the surrender of Fort Mackinac to British regulars, Canadian militia and Indians without so much as a fight. At the same time, Brigadier General William Hull, the governor of Michigan Territory, ran a disastrous campaign into Upper Canada that resulted in the surrender of Fort Detroit. Then Fort Dearborn on the southern tip of Lake Michigan, now Chicago, surrendered, with the occupants mostly massacred by Indians as they abandoned it.

After capturing Fort Detroit, Canadian forces under General Isaac Brock moved to counter the American invasion on the Niagara frontier. The Niagara River joins the southern end of Lake Ontario onto the easternmost

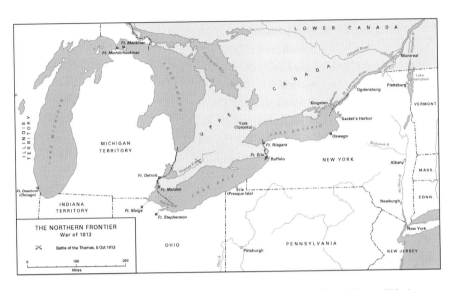

Map of the northern theater during the War of 1812. *Center for Military History, U.S. Army,* *http://www.history.army.mil/books/AMH/amh-toc.htm.*

tip of Lake Erie and is the boundary between the United States and Canada. Fort Niagara was located at the upper end of the Niagara River on the American side; opposite, on the Canadian side, was Fort George. Farther down, the Canadians had Queenston Heights on the opposite side of the river from Lewiston in the United States.

In a later attempt to recapture Fort Detroit in January 1813, a force of one thousand men under Brigadier General James Winchester met defeat at Frenchtown on the Raisin River twenty-six miles below Detroit. Besides the killing of one hundred and the capturing of five hundred Kentucky riflemen, many of the wounded Americans were massacred by the Indians who had accompanied the British, thus inspiring the rallying cry, "Remember the Raisin."

Canada's capital, York, lay on the other side of Lake Ontario opposite Fort Niagara. Toward the southern end of the Niagara River was Canada's Fort Erie; across the river was Niagara Falls and Buffalo, New York. During the Niagara campaign, the area around the Niagara River exploded with revenge-filled raids, as possession of territory changed hands from one side to the other.

American major general Stephen van Rensselaer, with his army at Lewiston, attempted to cross the river and scale three-hundred-foot cliffs to capture Queenston Heights. The failed attempt on October 12, 1813, cost three hundred American lives, with one thousand men captured. Brigadier General Alexander Smyth, who maintained a sizable American force at Buffalo and another at Fort Niagara upriver, hampered the effort by refusing Rensselaer's request for reinforcements.

Neither was Major General Henry Dearborn at Albany, 250 miles away, in the mood to engage his troops in that theater of war. However, by November 1812, he had sent a large force to Plattsburg, a key American base on the western shore of Lake Champlain, which borders both New York and Vermont. Dearborn, with an army of seven regiments of regulars, including artillery and dragoons, announced that he intended to lead his army from Plattsburg to Montreal, but his forces were driven back, with the Vermont and New York Militias refusing to cross the Canadian border.

Into this mêlée along the Canadian border were thrust Pittsylvania soldiers Lieutenant Samuel Hairston Jr. of the 20th Infantry and Lieutenant Walter Coles with the 2nd Regiment Light Dragoons. One month before the Battle of Queenston Heights along the Niagara River, Coles wrote home to his sister, Catherine, at Chalk Level on September 13, 1812, from a cavalry camp at Trenton, New Jersey. He indicated that he was leaving in a few days, and "[t]here are now upwards of three hundred men encamped here who are to march immediately. The 1st division will march tomorrow & the

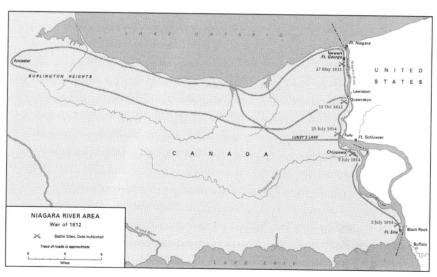

Map of the Niagara River corridor during the War of 1812. *Center for Military History, U.S. Army, http://www.history.army.mil/books/AMH/amh-toc.htm.*

second in 3 or 4 days afterward. I expect to remain but time enough to rest in Albany and get to Plattsburg some time in the end of October."

It is not evident what role Lieutenant Hairston played in this failed attempt at Montreal by General Dearborn. On November 7, 1812, he wrote home from Fairfax Court House, Virginia, to his father, Colonel George Hairston, reporting that "the Presidential Election terminated in this county [Fairfax] in favor of Jas Madison." However, Lieutenant Coles was probably with Dearborn's force; after the failed attempt at Montreal, he was encamped again at Danville, Vermont. From there, he wrote a letter to his sister on December 22 indicating that his last letter from her was two months old and that he had been busy with military writing. Both of the latter indicators make it more than likely that he had been with Dearborn's army.

Despite the setbacks in the invasion of Canada, Henry Clay, the Speaker of the House of Representatives, eloquently defended the war before Congress. In another memorable speech in January 1813, when the issue of increasing the size of the military came in the wake of the failures of the Canadian campaign, he was undeterred in his support of the war:

> *Haughty as she* [England] *is, we once triumphed over her, and if we do not listen to the councils of timidity and despair we shall again prevail. In such a cause, with the aid of Providence, we must come out crowned with success; but if we fail, let us fail like men…and expire together in one common struggle, fighting for seamen's rights and free trade.*

Yet while the land war against Canada was failing, notable American naval victories occurred at sea. In August 1812, the USS *Constitution* defeated the HMS *Guerriere* in a ferocious battle off the coast of Nova Scotia. With the enemy's cannonballs bouncing off the wooden sides of the *Constitution*, one of its sailors exclaimed that its sides were made of iron. "Old Ironsides" became the famous ship's moniker, and to this day, it has never lost a battle. It remains the oldest commissioned ship in the United States Navy.

Other similar naval victories helped improve morale over the failing Canadian campaign. While the war between America and Britain was a mismatch, the superiority of America's naval forces was due to experienced commanders, who had earned their stripes in the Barbary Wars with North African pirates during Jefferson's administration and in the Quasi War with France. In addition, the American navy was equipped with new heavy frigates (forty-four guns) that usually overpowered the normally equipped thirty-eight-gun British frigates.

The USS *Constitution* defeated the British warship HMS *Guerriere* on August 19, 1812. *Engraving by Marshall Johnson, U.S. Naval Heritage Command.*

In September 1813, Commodore Oliver Hazard Perry defeated a British force on Lake Erie that would give the Americans control of the lake and prevent the British from supplying troops in the Northwest. Perry's victory paved the way for General Harrison to march into Canada, where he defeated a force that included British and Indians at the Battle of the Thames on October 5, 1813, in which the Indian leader Tecumseh was killed.

Parallel in time with Harrison's victory in the Northwest and the American control of Lake Erie, naval and army encounters continued on the Niagara frontier and Upper Canada around Lake Ontario. Both the British and Americans engaged in a shipbuilding program on Lake Ontario, as water travel was the only practical means of transporting troops.

The British built up a naval base at Kingston, on the northern shore of the lake near the point where it connects to the St. Lawrence River. On the American side, Sacket's Harbor on the southern shore in New York provided a station for the American fleet.

In a renewed effort on the Niagara front, General Dearborn moved his troops from Plattsburg to Sacket's Harbor to join the American fleet under Commodore Isaac Chauncey. Plans were made for them to move to the opposite side of the lake and attack Kingston to destroy the British naval base there, but believing that the British were reinforcing Kingston, Dearborn opted to attack York (Toronto), the capital of Lower Canada. Unfortunately, on April 13, 1813, York's public buildings were burned and government records destroyed as a result of the American presence there. Although historians have generally concluded that the American forces didn't intend for this to happen, the mayhem at York did intensify the feelings of retaliation among the British.

On May 27, 1813, an amphibious landing sent Dearborn's four thousand troops in an attack against the British at Fort George on the northern end of the Niagara River. American forces under Colonel Winfield Scott forced the British to abandon Fort George, and this also led to the British abandoning other forts on the Canadian side of the Niagara River—Forts Chippewa, Queenston and Erie, near the lower end.

By December 10, 1813, the British had recaptured Fort George. In the process, the Americans burned Newark nearby, destroying 150 homes and turning the inhabitants, mostly women and children, out into freezing weather and snow. As war raged on the Niagara frontier, the British attacked and massacred Lewiston inhabitants on December 18 and then burned Buffalo, New York.

The British had also recaptured Fort Erie, but in early 1814, a renewed American attack once again recaptured the fort. After successfully doing so, the American army under Major General Jacob Brown advanced to the Chippewa River, where American forces under Brigadier General Winfield Scott repelled the British on July 5.

Another battle under Scott, at Lundy's Lane on July 25, was one of the hardest-fought battles and one of the bloodiest on the Niagara frontier, leaving both armies exhausted. The Americans withdrew to Fort Erie, but after a British siege in 1814, Americans destroyed the fort and crossed the Niagara to the U.S. side. By this time, the American army had improved its fighting ability but still failed to dominate the Niagara corridor in the effort to invade Canada from that direction.

Lieutenant Samuel Hairston of Pittsylvania County, according to Hairston family information, fought with Winfield Scott on the Niagara frontier. Letters written by him in August 1813 from Fort George, available from the Adjutant General's Office, suggest that Hairston saw action in Scott's capture of Fort George that May 1813 and that he was there when the British attempted to blockade the fort from July to October 1813 in their effort to retake it. More than likely, Hairston was with Dearborn's forces that had previously left Sacket's Harbor, captured York and then crossed Lake Ontario to Fort George.

At least two other Pittsylvania County soldiers, and no doubt others, were involved in the Niagara campaign. War Department records indicate that John Nichols enlisted on July 27, 1813, in the 20th Infantry and was discharged at Buffalo on May 31, 1815. Hardiman Stone, also of the county, joined the 24th Infantry on May 12, 1812, and was discharged in Buffalo in 1815. He was sick at Lewistown and also at Sacket's Harbor in July 1814.

While the Niagara frontier was embroiled in the back-and-forth struggles between the British and Americans, other activity was occurring on Lake Champlain. Early in the war, Lieutenant Thomas Macdonough was chosen to build and organize a navy presence on the lake whose primary purpose was to transport army troops between Plattsburg, New York, on the western shore to Burlington, Vermont, on the eastern shore.

In the meantime, the British were building ships and using Ile-aux-Noix, a small fortified British island about four miles or so north on the Richelieu River, as a naval support base. The Richelieu River flows from Lake Champlain and empties into the St. Lawrence. On June 3, 1813, two sloops, the USS *Growler* and the USS *Eagle*, sailed too far up the river and became trapped by the British. Lieutenant Walter Coles of the 2nd Light Dragoons evidently referred to this event in a letter written from his post at Burlington to his sister in Pittsylvania County, dated June 15, 1813:

I fear you have been alarmed for this post. It has been in great danger—the greatest depot of provisions ever in America has been exposed on the shores of the lake that is in command of the enemy—on the first day of this month we were in possession of three sloops and two gunboats, in all mounting thirty-six guns, the enemy had five gunboats but in an engagement between three gunboats and two of our sloops, they succeeded in capturing the sloops, which has given them complete command of the lake.

Macdonough had turned Burlington into a command post with military storehouses, munitions and guns. He had also purchased materials and vessels necessary to control the lake. That put Burlington in danger, as Coles noted in his first sentence in the previous quote. With the British in command of the lake for the moment, Lieutenant Coles noted:

It was supposed that the countrymen here would be bombarded immediately, and why it has not been done, I cannot imagine—Our barracks and all the military stores might have been burnt but it is too late now, several pieces of cannon have arrived, and many large pieces will

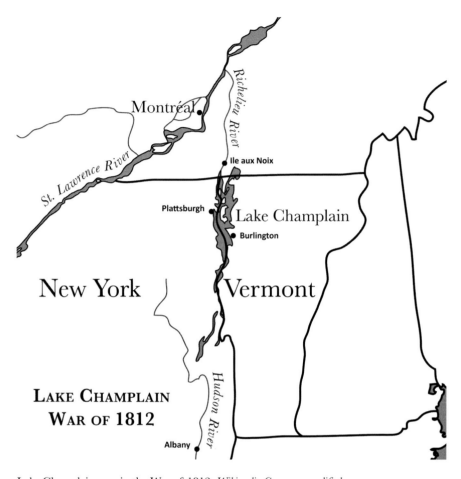

Lake Champlain area in the War of 1812. *Wikimedia Commons, modified.*

> *come in today, so not only to form a Battery, but to arm sloops enough to service the command of the lake.*

Coles then noted that two regiments 1,600 strong had been sent there and that "five hundred of our regiment came yesterday from Bennington. About six hundred of the other regiment will be in today—This increase of forces will make this army together with the frontier posts quite formidable." He then added:

> *On the eighth of the month I was ordered to bear a flag of truce to the Isle au Noire [sic] with dispatches from the secretary of war to the governor of*

Canada. I sailed down the lake accordingly but was stopped two miles and a half on the other side of the line—I wrote to the commanding officer of the Isle au Noire [sic] informing him of my business and in three hours was waited on by a major and two lieutenants of the Prince Regent's regiment.—They were elegant gentlemen and treated me very politely.

As the year progressed, one of the worst moments of the war occurred in the Montreal/St. Lawrence theater. An attempted two-pronged attack against Montreal failed miserably. James Wilkinson, commanding six thousand American troops at Sacket's Harbor, was to proceed in ships from there to Montreal and attack the city from the western side.

Major General Wade Hampton started from Burlington, Vermont, in mid-September with 5,400 men and headed for Plattsburg. From there, he planned to proceed north up Lake Champlain, follow the Richelieu River to the St. Lawrence and then attack Montreal across the river. Changing course, he took up a defensive position along the Chateauguay River. There he was turned back by a smaller force of 1,700 Canadian militia, regulars and Indians on October 25. He then refused to join Wilkinson and retreated back to Plattsburg.

Elbridge Gerry Jr. addressed a letter to Miss Catherine Coles on October 17, 1813, a few days before the defeat at the Battle of Chateauguay. He had previously returned from his visit to Pittsylvania County with his cousin and her brother, Walter, who evidently had been on furlough before he returned to Hampton's army. They rode horses back to Fredericksburg, Virginia, and then took the stage to Philadelphia, from which Walter proceeded to Burlington.

Gerry wrote the following about Walter and the war: "The latest account we have of General Hampton left him at or near Osdenburgh [Ogdensburg, located down the St. Lawrence River parallel to Plattsburg]. It is presumed they intend to either attack Montreal, or to cooperate with the other armies & make a descent on Kingston." As if to alleviate Catherine's anxiety about her brother's situation, Gerry added:

The dragoons I believe are all with H. but in battle they have seldom anything to do, until the retreat of the enemy, & then they pursue & consequently are in very little danger if and, for a vanquished foe, are wholly engaged in saving their own lives, & not in taking the lives of others which is confirmed in this invasion.… These remarks show that my valuable friend Walter, will be very safe in battle, & will gain glory at a less risk than his fellow officers, on foot. I think my dear Catherine, that you have but little occasion for anxiety should Walter be engaged.

Gerry then encouraged her with good news that had happened the month before: "Our gallant Perry on Lake Erie has captured the whole British fleet, whose force was inferior to that of the enemy. This is the first fleet that England has lost for a century." He ended his letter by noting Harrison's victory over Governor General Proctor's army, which had also taken place at the Battle of the Thames in Canada the month before. Harrison's victory was a direct result of Perry's victory on Lake Erie, which had left the British unable to provide tactical or logistical support to Proctor's army:

He has taken all Proctor's army, indians, officers, & every person or thing, except Proctor himself, who escaped, but is closely pursued. This is the first good victory our army has obtained on the frontier. I think it decides the fate of poor Canada. This is an army distinct from Walters, and I expect it will render easy, a victory, on his side. All the dragoons are with Gen H, & in a few days we must hear of his success. You have less reason to fear for Walter now, because the Indians and Canadians will join us, so we can conquer almost without fighting.

Time would show that Gerry's optimism was overreaching about taking Canada, but at least he offered the comfort of his words to reassure Catherine, far away in Pittsylvania County, of her brother Walter's safety.

The month after Gerry wrote that letter, on November 11, 1813, General Wilkinson, with eight thousand infantry, 150 gunboats and twenty-four guns but without any support from Hampton, suffered a defeat against a sizable British force at Chrysler's Farm, situated along the St. Lawrence, halfway to Montreal. The Montreal campaign was abandoned, and Wilkinson made winter quarters at French Mills, New York. One Pittsylvania County soldier in the 20th Infantry, Thomas Walker, age twenty-three, had enlisted on May 26, 1812, and was discharged at French Mills on November 30, 1813, after Wilkinson's retreat there.

Unable to gather supplies, many in Wilkinson's army fell sick, with 450 in a hospital in Malone, New York, about twenty miles away and many others at French Mills. National Archives records indicate that Charles Nichols, William Parson and Hansen Regney, all born in Pittsylvania County, had enlisted in the U.S. Army in 1813 and that all died in Malone,

New York. Elijah Hamilton, a twenty-one-year-old farmer who enlisted on June 8, 1812, was sick at the hospital in Malone from February 19, 1814, to January 26, 1815.

Wilkinson moved his army to Plattsburg and then, on March 30, 1814, moved them to New York and Burlington, Vermont. In a final attempt to accomplish a victory, Wilkinson advanced to battle at Lacolle Mills, just inside the Canadian border. However, his force was repulsed with the help of British gunboats and soldiers from the Ile-aux-Noix.

Pittsylvania County soldiers in that theater of war, being so far from home, had to have been discouraged at the turn of events, the failure of Wilkinson's and Hampton's leadership and, most especially, the failure of a successful invasion of Canada. They could not have known that the British would next turn the tables and seek to invade the United States, although their efforts, too, would ultimately fail.

Chapter 6
THE BATTLE OF CRANEY ISLAND

*This inferior force, in the face of a formidable naval armament…repelled the
enemy with considerable loss.*
—*Brigadier General Robert Taylor, commander of Virginia Militia
at Norfolk, 1813*

In early 1813, the British, in the attempt to divert attention from Canada
and take the offensive, blockaded the Chesapeake Bay. The blockade
lasted to the end of the war, with the British marauding at will up and down
the bay. With only inexperienced militia, shore batteries and gunboats for
protection, Chesapeake citizens were at the mercy of the invaders' veteran
troops and big warships.

Vice Admiral Sir John Warren had been appointed commander-in-chief
of British forces in Halifax, the West Indies and the whole coast of America,
with major bases in Halifax and Bermuda. His subordinate, Rear Admiral
Sir George Cockburn, became his chief lieutenant in prosecuting British
intentions in the bay.

Cockburn had been in the navy since age nine, when he was a captain's
servant and had spent more time on sea than land. Over the next two
years around the Chesapeake Bay, he would come to be despised due to his
harsh treatment of Chesapeake inhabitants. It's telling that even Napoleon,
whom Cockburn had transported to St. Helena, described him as "rough,
overbearing, [and] vain."

The blockade began in February 1813 after Admiral Sir John Warren's
declaration of a "strict and rigorous blockade" the previous December.

Not even ships from neutral countries were allowed to depart the bay. In early March 1813, Admiral Cockburn established his anchorage just off Lynnhaven Bay, near the entrance to Chesapeake Bay. Initially bypassing Norfolk nearby, his squadron of ships penetrated the upper bay, terrorizing it in every way possible. Admiral Warren had instructed them to "chastise the Americans into submission."

That sentiment, echoed in the *London Evening Star* that previous September 1813, appeared to represent the typical British attitude toward the Americans:

> *All the prating about maritime rights, with which the Americans have recently nauseated the ears of every cabinet minister in Europe must be silenced by the strong and manly voice of reason…America must be BEATEN INTO SUBMISSION! The law of nations have been always the law of the strongest—England is, therefore the DICTATOR of the maritime laws of the civilized world, and long may she retain her superiority!*

With such an unbridled claim to the sea, the British did not hesitate to impose their own brand of justice on the Chesapeake. In their attempt to do so, the British destroyed government stores, harbors and shipping and engaged in skirmishes with America militia, captured numerous vessels, interrupted trade and employed themselves in other atrocities. They especially ransacked farms for provisions. In *The Battle of Craney Island*, by John Hallahan, we read of the rich opportunity provided by the bay for the British to supply themselves:

> *It was one of the most important commercial highways of the era, carrying manufactured goods, produce, and passengers to and from Richmond, Washington, Baltimore, and Havre de Grace and thence to points north and west. Its farms were ripe with livestock, vegetables and fruit. Potable water abounded and game and seafood of the greatest variety and utmost delicacy were easily obtained. It was a provisioning officer's dream come true.*

There was a heavy price to pay if resistance was offered. In one instance, Havre de Grace, Maryland, a town of sixty houses, experienced the wrath of a British attack. The British shelled the village and used Congreve rockets to create complete chaos. Many homes were ransacked, demolished and set on fire, along with the destruction of ferryboats, a sawmill, a blacksmith shop, stables and haystacks.

Barber Badger, in *The Naval Temple*, published in 1816, wrote that the British, before returning back down the Chesapeake Bay, wreaked havoc on what were mostly defenseless communities. "The destruction committed by the British in these places, was wanton in the extreme. The houses were set on fire. The furniture and other property of the inhabitants were either destroyed or conveyed on board their vessels."

Even though Cockburn had initially concentrated his attacks on the upper bay, Norfolk had continual fears of an attack on the town. In response, Norfolk had prepared for possible action with artillery batteries, redoubts and earthworks as the town and surrounding area filled up with troops of the U.S. Army and Virginia militia. Norfolk had not forgotten the time the USS *Chesapeake* was attacked by the HMS *Leopard* off its shores in 1807. Then the town was outraged and ready for war, but now, with the British in control of the bay, the citizens would be on the defensive.

The town was defended by Forts Nelson and Norfolk, both of which lay on opposite sides of the Elizabeth River, which separated Norfolk and Portsmouth. The British considered Norfolk the "center of maritime resistance" for the Chesapeake Bay, so its importance was without question. A defeat at Norfolk would be a blow to the whole region. Norfolk would also become a British station to receive British forces coming from Bermuda.

Stuart Butler, in the National Archives *Prologue* article "Defending Norfolk," stressed that "Norfolk was an important port. Cotton, flour, and tobacco were shipped from there to points around the world. Although it ranked below New York, Boston, Philadelphia, and Baltimore in overall foreign trade, it was still important for trade and its strategic location."

This commercial activity at Norfolk also encouraged its shipbuilding industry. The USS *Chesapeake* was launched there in 1799, and in 1800, the navy chose Gosport, a short distance from Portsmouth, as one of six federal shipyards. The capture of Norfolk and Portsmouth would constitute a serious threat to Gosport Naval Yard. The shipyard had been previously captured and destroyed during the American Revolution in 1779, with all the ships and tobacco in Portsmouth taken as well.

The frigate USS *Constellation*, which usually anchored between the forts, was also a prime target of the British. Casually known as the "Yankee Race Horse," the thirty-eight-gun frigate had distinguished itself in engagements with Barbary pirates during Jefferson's administration and the Quasi War with France. The day after Christmas 1812, with more than three hundred crewmen, it sailed down the Potomac River to Annapolis for some repairs. Afterward, it headed down the Chesapeake Bay toward the sea.

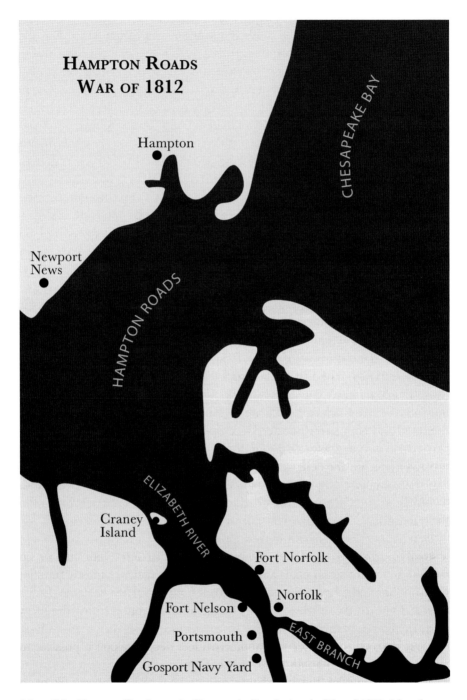

Map of the Hampton Roads area in Chesapeake Bay during the War of 1812. *Map after original from the Society of the War of 1812.*

However, before it could leave the bay, the ship had been forced into the Elizabeth River near Norfolk that February due to the British blockade. Should the British capture the *Constellation*, it would become a prize trophy in England, especially after the series of resounding triumphs of American ships over the British on the high seas.

Norfolk had already had its trade cut off and its shipping bottled up during the Embargo of 1807. Now in the spring of 1813, with the British blockade across the mouth of the Chesapeake Bay, the town's trade was again cut off, with every reason to expect the British to pay a visit.

The blockade itself was damaging enough. In 1811, Virginia exports were valued at $4.8 million but would drop to $17,581 by 1814, a precipitous decline already underway by the time the British focused on Norfolk. Since agricultural products and other goods were once again denied export, Pittsylvania County and its agricultural products would have been especially hard hit.

By mid-June 1813, Admiral Cockburn's British forces had returned to his headquarters at Lynnhaven Bay from its forays in the Upper Chesapeake. Admiral Warren was also back in the bay with the additional British army units under the command of Colonel Sydney Beckwith. Counting marines and sailors, Warren had a sizable force of nearly five thousand men.

Although Warren's goal was Norfolk, he knew that Craney Island, which guarded the approach to the Elizabeth River, was the key to the capture of the town and navy yard. Back in December 26, 1808, during the embargo, Thomas Newton wrote to the governor that fortifications needed to be erected there "for the defence of Norfolk and Portsmouth." He stressed that "Norfolk is a point of great importance. It is the Key to the Chesapeake Bay, a middle station between the Northern and Southern States." Thus, the need to fortify Craney Island became a high priority early on.

Defending Craney Island looked difficult, but it had advantages. It was a small and flat oblong island of about thirty or so acres with little or no vegetation except scrub pines and some underbrush. It was mostly mudflat and sandbar and a haven for nesting herons (cranes), hence its name. It was oriented toward the northwest, with the mainland about four hundred feet from the island, with the water four to five feet deep between them at high tide. At low tide, the water was about two feet deep, making it possible to wade as well as ride a horse across to the island.

The south end of the island was oriented toward Lambert's Point, a peninsula of land on the opposite side of the mouth of the Elizabeth River. Craney Island's shallow waters or flats also extended into Hampton Roads for about two miles, thus preventing any large ships from supporting an amphibious assault.

Despite Admiral Warren's large British force, his subordinate, Admiral Cockburn, sadly underestimated the fight before him as the British planned their attack on the island. He is quoted by the *Niles' Weekly Register* as boasting to his troops, "We will storm Fort Nelson and be in Norfolk to supper and there you will have three days' plunder and the free use of a number of fine women."

With such anticipation before them, no wonder the officers brought shaving gear, picnic baskets and pet dogs with them on the barges when they assaulted the island. In *The Battle of Craney Island*, the author indicates that the British were hoping for "one of Cockburn's easy Chesapeake Bay victories where an ill-trained militia would fire a few desultory rounds and then melt away before superior redcoat strength."

This time, British tactics didn't work. The men on Craney Island were in no mood to back down. Even though the defenders faced the prospect of being surrounded and isolated on the island, it proved no deterrent. The men on Craney Island were ready for a fight.

Admiral Warren planned a joint operation with about 2,500 army and navy forces operating in unison to possess the island and then moving up the Elizabeth River to attack Fort Norfolk, subsequently taking Norfolk, Portsmouth and the naval yard, along with the *Constellation*. Admiral Cockburn's naval assault would attack the island from the northeast, or the side facing the bay waters, and Colonel Beckwith's troops would attack from the mainland, crossing over to the island at the same time from the southwest.

With the British experience of continually scattering and routing militia units up and down the Chesapeake Bay and its tributary rivers, they logically assumed that a Craney Island defeat was an accomplished fact, a matter of going through the motions. And the numbers of American defenders would seem to have supported that belief.

General Robert Taylor, in command of troops in the Fifth Military District, reported afterward that his whole force at the time of the battle "consisted of 50 riflemen, 446 infantry of the line, 91 state artillery, and 150 seamen and marines [from the *Constellation*] furnished by Captain Tarbell. Of these, 43 were on the sick list." All together, this was not a sizable force to match British veterans, most of whom had battle experience from the Napoleonic Wars. Nor were the American gunboats that blocked the Elizabeth River any real match for the British warships.

A map of Craney Island circa 1813 (included with this text) shows cannon batteries lined up behind breastworks on the western end of the island, with Colonel Beatty's 4th Virginia Regiment behind the breastworks; toward the end of the breastworks is stationed Lieutenant Colonel Thomas Reade's 1st Artillery Regiment. On the easterly end of the island is an unfinished fort. The side of the island toward the mainland has a bridge that exits onto the island behind Colonel Beatty's Regiment. Behind the breastworks, the map shows a flag staff and magazine.

Both Lieutenant Colonel Beatty and Lieutenant Colonel Reade Jr.'s regiment were constituted by order of the Virginia adjutant general about six weeks prior to the battle at Craney Island. Reade's artillery regiment existed as a command from April to October 1813. Under his command were several companies from various counties, including King and Queen, Charlotte, Loudon, Berkeley, Norfolk and Norfolk Borough.

Also included was Captain Samuel Calland's company of artillery from Pittsylvania County. Brigadier General Robert Taylor, writing to the

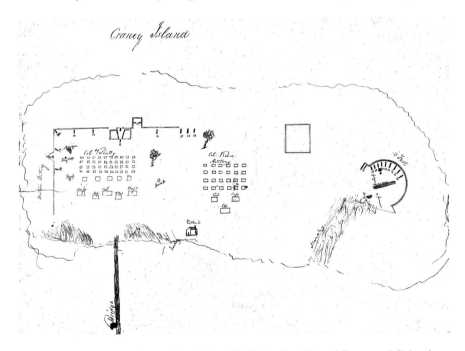

Military installations on Craney Island, circa 1813, showing Colonel Beatty and Colonel Reade's Virginia Militia regiments. *Small Special Collections Library, University of Virginia.*

governor on April 24, 1813, from Norfolk, noted that "Capt. Callond's [*sic*] artillery arrived several days ago, and three transports have just arrived in the harbor."

The map of Craney Island was likely made after the battle, when the island's defenses were reinforced to withstand further attacks. Various companies of Colonel Reade's artillery regiment were at Craney Island during the battle, but Calland's company is not listed in a morning report of troops under his command the day of the battle. Calland's company of artillery was probably at Fort Nelson, across the Elizabeth River from Fort Norfolk. Nobody was sure where the British would strike in the area around Norfolk, so adequate attention had to be paid to sites other than the island.

Samuel Calland Jr. was the son of the Scottish immigrant Samuel Calland, after whom the Callands area off Route 57 in Pittsylvania County is named. The senior Calland operated a store at the site of the first county courthouse in colonial days.

In August 1807, just two months after the *Chesapeake-Leopard* affair, Samuel Calland Jr. qualified as an artillery officer. In a typical fashion for militia officers, the court record reads, "Samuel Calland Jun produced a commission from his Excellency the Governor appointing him Second Lieutenant in a Company of Artillery in the first Division and first Regiment of the militia of Virginia and took the oath by law prescribed." By 1810, he was qualified as captain over the company.

In Samuel Calland's company was Edmund Gross, an eighteen-year-old farmer, who said in his pension application that he was discharged while encamped at Craney Island on October 14, 1813. Another member was Samuel Mitchell, a twenty-six-year-old farmer when he enlisted at Callands in late March 1813 and this author's third-great-grandfather. In his pay vouchers, he is listed as being at Fort Norfolk from April through July ranked as second corporal and then from August through October 14 as first corporal, at which time he was discharged while encamped at Craney Island.

Obviously, then, Calland's Pittsylvania artillery company was stationed at Craney Island after the battle. Its presence and that of other units acted as a defense against any follow-up visits by the British.

The following narrative, paraphrased and condensed (with some exceptions), appeared in the July 1848 *Virginia Historical Register* and was quoted in *War in the Lower Chesapeake and Hampton Roads Areas*. The narrative was a firsthand account from an officer involved in the Craney Island battle, which occurred on June 22, 1813.

M | **6 Art'y.** (Read, Jr.'s.) | **Va. Militia.**

Samuel Mitchell

1 Corp'l., { Capt. Samuel Calland's Company, 6 Reg't Virginia Militia Artillery. (**War of 1812.**)

Appears on

Company Pay Roll

for _____ *Aug 1 to Oct 14*, 181*3* .

Roll dated _____ *Oct 14*, 181*3* .

Commencement of service or of this settlement, } *Aug 1*, 181*3* .

Expiration of service or of this settlement, } *Oct 14*, 181*3* .

Distance from place of discharge home, *280*

Term of service charged, *2* months, *28* days.

Pay per month, _____ *10* dollars, _____ cents.

Amount of pay, _____ *29* dollars, *33* cents.

Remarks: _____

_____

_____

_____

_____

_____

_____

_____

_____

_____

(572)   *Crosby* / Copyist

M | **6 Art'y.** (Read, Jr.'s.) | **Va. Militia.**

Samuel Mitchell

1 Corp'l., { Capt. Samuel Calland's Company of the Artillery Regiment, Virginia Militia, commanded by Lieut. Col. Thomas Read, Jr. (**War of 1812.**)

Appears on

Company Muster Roll

for _____ *Aug 1 to Oct 14*, 181*3* .

Roll dated *at encampment on Craney Island Oct 14* 181*3* .

Date of appointment or when last mustered, } *Aug 1*, 181*3* .

To what time engaged, _____ *Oct 14*, 181*3* .

Distance from place of discharge home, *280 miles*

Present or absent, *Present*

Remarks: _____

_____

_____

_____

_____

_____

_____

_____

_____

[569]   *Crosby* / Copyist.

Muster roll and company pay roll of Samuel Mitchell, corporal in Captain Samuel Calland's artillery company. *National Archives and Records Administration, Pension Files for War of 1812, Marvin Osborne.*

The letter's author relates that on June 21, enemy ships proceeded up Hampton Roads and anchored off the mouth of the Nansemond River about two miles from the island. The British convoy consisted of fifteen to twenty vessels made up of ships of the line, along with frigates and transports. At dawn on the twenty-second, the enemy's boats (barges) were seen passing back and forth from ship to shore. On the island, artillery, infantry and riflemen, joined by the sailors from the *Constellation*, lined up on the west side.

The letter writer expressed the enthusiasm of the defenders:

> *Every arrangement being made to defend the post, we waited the approach of the enemy and felt that we were prepared to give him a decent reception, for the troops were full of ardor. The next thing was to let the enemy see what flag we intended to fight under. As we had no flag staff, a long pole was got, to which the "Star Spangled Banner" was nailed, the pole planted in the breastwork, and the Stars and Stripes floated in the breeze.*

The fact that the flag was nailed up made it impossible to pull down, indicating that the men on the island had no intention of surrendering.

The British barges landed 2,500 infantry and marines on the beach on the mainland across from the upper part of Craney Island and formed a line of march that disappeared into the trees. It was believed that they might be marching to Portsmouth to take possession of the town and also destroy Gosport Naval Yard.

From behind a house on the mainland, the British began shooting Congreve rockets at the island, but to no avail. The island's defenders dislodged the British by firing grape and canister shot into the house. Shock and awe was the greatest contribution of the Congreve rockets in the war. A newspaper article from March 10, 1813, added to the hysteria around them by referring to the rockets as the "most terrific instrument of destruction which has ever been discovered since the invention of gunpowder." Once ignited, they were good for three hundred to five hundred yards in five or ten seconds, but they were horribly inaccurate and were more noted for their fireworks than firepower.

At the same time the British were attempting to attack from the mainland, they were also approaching the island on the bay side. Admiral Warren's ornate barge the *Centipede*—which was fifty feet long, with thirty-four oars and a three-pounder brass cannon on the bow—led the flotilla of barges into the waters fronting Craney Island.

Our letter writer of 1848 explained that the Virginia artillery waited until it was in close range and then delivered a "brisk and heavy fire of grape and canister." The enemy continued to advance until the *Centipede* and headmost boats were grounded in the shallow mudflats, forcing the other barges to halt their advance. "So quick and galling was our fire they were thrown into the greatest confusion, and commenced a hasty retreat." Sailors assisting with artillery hauled the *Centipede* to the shore, and it was later sent to the Gosport Naval Yard.

The enemy's loss was estimated by some Virginia newspapers at two hundred killed, wounded and captured. Twenty-two prisoners were said to have been taken on the beach, and twenty-five to thirty deserters (most, if not all, Frenchmen) reportedly came to the island as well. However, Admiral Warren later wrote, "I am happy to say the loss in the above affair has not been considerable, and only two boats sunk." It is difficult to say how many casualties the British suffered, but other documentation makes it more likely that sixteen were killed, with fifty-two missing.

No Americans were killed in battle, but a sentinel guarding the ammunition powder stored in a tent on the beach was found dead outside the fort, stripped of his clothes, his left arm ripped nearly off and black all over as much as the powder could make him. For some unknown reason, the powder exploded, and the sound was heard around the island and even at Norfolk, which further frightened its inhabitants.

When Virginia militia units finally waded to the mainland after the battle, they saw sheep and hogs "wantonly shot," and "at the house of an old widow lady her furniture was broken, beds cut and feathers thrown into the yard, and such like heroic deeds, becoming a swinish and sheepish enemy."

The humiliation of the British from being severely beaten by such a small force of militia and sailors no doubt motivated them to attack the village of Hampton on the north shore of Hampton Roads on June 25, 1813. The 400 American militia there were no match for the 2,500 British invaders. The soldiers were reputedly promised "booty and beauty" and in consequence destroyed a large amount of property and committed other "inhuman and shocking acts." In a diary kept by one of the British officers there, he even wrote:

> *Every horror was perpetrated with impunity—rape, pillage, murder—and not a man was punished…. Strong is my dislike to what is, perhaps a necessary part of our job, viz., plundering and ruining the peasantry. We drive all their cattle, and of course ruin them. My hands are clean; but it is hateful to see the poor Yankees robbed, and to be the robber.*

Women were "abused in the most shameful manner" by soldiers and by escaped slaves, who were "encouraged in their excesses." A poor bedridden man already near death was shot and killed in his bed, and his wife was wounded trying to protect him. His dog was killed as well.

The atrocities were blamed mostly on the Independent Company of Foreigners, often incorrectly referred to as the Chasseurs Britanniques. These soldiers were French prisoners from the Napoleonic Wars who chose to fight alongside the British instead of enduring life as prisoners of war in Spain or Portugal. They were dismissed from British service after Hampton and never used again.

Hampton was of no strategic value, so the British did not remain there. However, like other terrorist activities by the British up and down the Chesapeake Bay, the Hampton Raid created unparalleled hatred for the British army and navy.

The Craney Island victory was the Virginia Militia's finest hour. The American garrison defeated a "massive amphibious assault by seasoned British troops." Dr. Philip Barraud of Norfolk wrote to Lieutenant Colonel John Cocke that "Craney Island with 600 men and fifteen gunboats have saved our town against 22 ships of sail of the best description and a land force of men near 3000."

General Taylor wrote to the secretary of war on July 4, 1813, about the battle: "The courage and constancy with which this inferior force, in the face of a formidable naval armament, not only sustained a position in which nothing was complete, but repelled the enemy with considerable loss, cannot fail to inspire the approbation of their government and the applause of their country."

The threat around Norfolk subsided for a time, but it would be renewed in 1814, when the British received more reinforcements from those who served in the Napoleonic Wars. However, the bravery of the defenders of Craney Island and continued vigilance on the part of future militia and U.S. Army regulars in the area ensured that Norfolk was not the victim of a direct attack again.

Besides Captain Samuel Calland's Pittsylvania artillery company being stationed in Norfolk and Craney Island months after the battle, other men from Pittsylvania county militia companies and some Pittsylvanians who belonged to U.S. Army units were also stationed in and around Norfolk in the months to come.

Many militiamen served just six months and those in the army even longer. Most did not see any action. On the other hand, their presence was necessary. Stuart Butler, in his *Defending the Old Dominion*, related, "The Virginia Militia saw little action at Norfolk after the summer of 1813. By assembling and organizing large numbers of soldiers in the Norfolk area, however, Virginia's militia did show they could insure that no major British invasion force could land and be sustained very long."

Thus, the presence of Pittsylvania County soldiers did their part in preventing further loss and devastation by the British in a strategic area of operations around Norfolk and Portsmouth, where they could have been able to gain a foothold in the Old Dominion. The loss of Norfolk and the Gosport Naval Yard would have been a major disaster for the nation and no doubt would have substantially affected the outcome of the war.

Chapter 7
HOME AWAY FROM HOME

I have pretty well got used to the hardship of camp.
—*Second Lieutenant Walter Coles, cavalry camp in New Jersey, 1812*

C amp life for many of the army and militia soldiers was their first contact with war, and due to the hardships of being in the field or a strange environment during their tour of duty, war was not the glory road they might have envisioned. Defending the nation's honor involved more than just being in harm's way during battle.

U.S. Army soldiers like Walter Coles and Samuel Hairston and Virginia militiamen found camp life disconcerting since they were away from home, most often for the first time. General Robert Taylor, commander of the Fifth Military District around Norfolk, initiated a policy of separating men from the various called-up county militia companies that arrived and put them with different units. The men might have a new regimental and even a new company commander after they arrived on the field.

Being separated from home a great deal of the time, it was natural for soldiers to think of home. Their letters to those at home focused on conditions in camp but also the health of the family left behind, the condition of the farm that most had left and related issues. Responses from home tempered the heartache of being away.

From his letters to his sister, Catherine, back in Pittsylvania County, Lieutenant Walter Coles of Pittsylvania County had obviously never endured the military life. In his letter dated September 13, 1812, from Trenton, New Jersey, Coles gave a stark description of camp life, stating, "I have been encamped near Trenton for about 13 days & have got pretty well used to the hardship of a camp."

After commenting that there were only a few officers in camp, he elaborated on living conditions, attempting to put a positive face on the situation:

Each Capt has a tent to himself—& these tents we put our trunks in. We sleep upon mattresses laid upon planks which are rested on four low posts drove in the Ground. This is a very luxurious way of reposing which a march will not admit of. Our tables consist of wide planks placed (so as to be taken off) on large post fixed between the beds which can serve as chairs. We live in one general mess we take it by turns to be caterers, make our servants cook and send to market every morning with which sort of management we live very comfortably and cheaply.

Although Trenton, New Jersey, was famous as the site of General George Washington's dramatic victory during the American Revolution, it is obvious from Coles's writing that Trenton was not a place that neither he nor others in camp enjoyed. He wrote, "We have no society with the citizens of Trenton which I think a most inhospitable place. There ladies every evening walk about the camp but in consequence of the little attention paid to the officers by the citizens we never pay them any in camp."

One incident with the officers stands out, and he included it in his letter to Catherine:

The officers I have seen in my Regiment are very Gentiel [sic] young men excepting one or two—a First Lieut by the name of Chew from Philidelphie [sic] has been [a] diversion for us for some time. He staid in my tent. The other officers frequently assembled there to laugh at him for his vainly and pompous appearance. He is a young man who has seen much gentiel company, has read a good deal, but is extremely weak and nebulous. He was so frequently laughed at in my tent that it goes by the name of the critics tent. Mr. Chew has been so much teased that he has resigned & gone back to his parents under the pretense of ill health but to his eternal disgrace.

After leaving Trenton, Coles's station at Danville, Vermont, seemed more agreeable:

In this country people are all in one class of society and mainly on a level as to fortune, no pride of nobility or absence of money prevents matrimony. The girls are universally industrious, they milk cows, makeup bed & etc. A young man far from thinking a wife an expence marries a girl and makes a profitable bargain of it—therefore there are no old bachelors or old maids and it is thought not creditable to remain single after the common age of getting married.

Then he described the town:

Danville is a very cold destination, it is on the top of the Green mountain and surrounded with magnificent prospects of mountains covered with snow. The White Mountains of New Hampshire are at a great distance, but towering high unto the clouds are grand beyond description.

And again he offered a glimpse of camp life:

The county around here is exceedingly cheap, board in private houses is eight & six pence per week, but Capt Hall & myself being a mile from the village keep bachelors house, and since the frequent guests we are obliged to entertain, to return the civilities of the good people of Danville makes our expences amount to three or four dollars each week.

Instead of sleeping on the ground, as we did from the time we arrived at Platsburg till the time we left that place I now sleep on a plank raised on a frame and in a blanket wrapped in a large buffalo skin: this way of sleeping I like so well and having been so much accustomed to, that I should sleep badly in any feather bed in Virginia.

In April 1813, Walter Coles was stationed at Derby, Vermont. He wrote to Catherine about his dragoons disrupting the ongoing smuggling across the border and searching for a deserter but also the disagreeable nature of Derby: "Swenton is about 30 miles below Burlington on Lake Champlain, there are some hundred troops stationed there and although that is not a very agreeable place, yet I would go anywhere to get rid of the place and service that I am in." His complaints seemed more understandable with his comments about the "want of provisions" and the mention that "[o]n the first day of April the snow was four feet deep."

There is little doubt that having been raised in southern Virginia, far from such scenery, Lieutenant Walter Coles was experiencing more than just the war. He was being exposed to a different world than what he was used to.

Still, while adjusting to camp life, Lieutenant Coles often thought of home. On December 22, 1812, three days before Christmas, Lieutenant

Walter Coles wrote to Catherine again: "My Dear Sister, I am quite uneasy that I do not hear from home; my last dates from Virginia are more than two months old, and it is uncertain when these northern mails will bring me a letter, than which nothing would be a higher treat." Then he added:

I have so many letters to write and so much writing of a military sort that I neglected to write to the boys. I wish you would inform me where they are and what they are doing, ask all three to write to me...John and Bob I expect are doing well. I will thank you to insist upon their writing to me. I should be exceedingly pleased to receive a letter from my dear Mary.

Coles's June 15, 1813 letter to her indicates that he hadn't forgotten about the farm: "From the hostile situation off the coast of Virginia I was astonished at the sell [*sic*] of my Father's tobacco; but the crop was not as large as I expected—I suppose that the cultivation of tobacco has been greatly neglected since the declaration of war."

Contact with home was important, but rank and promotion were important to men on the battlefield, and Coles was no exception. The following story about twenty-two-year-old Walter Coles probably rang true for other young men of his day. He had been anxious for an independent command and promotion since the beginning of his service when he was appointed second lieutenant in March 1812. Yet he wrote from "Near Chalk Level, Pittsylvania March 30, 1812," with the following grudging acceptance of his commission:

Sir, I have received your letter of notification that I have been appointed a Second Lieutenant of Light Dragoons. Although the rank is lower than my friends and myself expected; yet...that it is more honorable to be promoted for merit than to be appointed by the influence of a representative in Congress who of young men can have but little acquaintance.

However, in a letter dated October 5, 1812, President Madison's secretary, Edward Coles, kindly addressed a letter to his and Walter's cousin Dolley Madison: "May I ask the favor of you to say to Mr. Madison that Walter Coles, who is now a second Lieut. in the Cavalry, has written to me that a first Lieut. of his battalion has resigned, and he wishes to be considered an applicant to fill the vacancy." Unfortunately, Walter Coles did not receive a promotion then, cousin or not. It was not until March 10, 1814, that

Letter from Walter Coles I, dated March 30, 1812, concerning his appointment as second lieutenant in the U.S. Light Dragoons. *Letters Received by the Adjutant General's Office, Record Group 94, National Archives and Records Administration, Stuart Butler.*

President James Madison recommended Walter Coles be promoted from second lieutenant to captain of a rifle company.

Elbridge Gerry Jr. took notice of Coles's elevation in rank and wrote to Catherine Coles in Pittsylvania on June 4, 1814: "I am informed that a captain's commission of the rifle corps has been conferred on him, & this I believe is a promotion that was desired. Should the war continue through the season, his service will probably be called for on the southern seaboard, as the enemy threaten to leave no point unvisited."

The desire for promotion was part of the glory of war as much as the chance to distinguish oneself in the heat of battle, but Walter Coles would not join the fight in the South. In six months, the war would be over. In less than a year, Coles would be discharged from the military, his home away from home, and return to Pittsylvania County. In the meantime, he and others had to deal with the less glorious issues of war.

Besides the issues regarding camp conditions, the desire of letters from home and concern over rank, other issues with military life included sickness and disease, desertion and dishonorable behavior.

Disease and sickness were major causes for depleting both the militia and the army. More men died in the War of 1812 from disease than as casualties of battle. Of the twenty thousand men who died in the war, only about one-quarter died from bullets. "Military Medicine in the War of 1812," an article on PBS.org, lists types of disease and sickness rampant in camps: typhoid, pneumonia, malaria, measles, smallpox, dysentery, food poisoning and diarrhea. In a hospital in Burlington, Vermont, where Walter Coles was stationed, an epidemic of infection killed seventy-five residents in one month. Walter Coles found himself in a similar situation at Danville, Vermont. He wrote home:

> *The hardships I have under gone have been a great service to me, while many men died, I* [illegible] *either from greater care over superior constitution at* [illegible] *we had no tents and the dragoons encamping in the night, had to settle on a flat below the hill; very much like the flat in the woods below the house & towards the plantation at home. The land was full of little hollows and the men drank and watered their horses. The officers and men all faired alike, many died and a great proportion of the army were taken sick at Platsburg & Burlington.*

In another letter from Woodstock, Virginia, dated December 14, 1814, to the Adjutant and Inspector General's Office in Washington, Captain Walter Coles wrote that

> *two men Ezekiel Peterson and Edward McClellan were left with me by Capt. Carrington as unfit for service on account of being ruptured—Peterson is now very* [sick]*...I do not think he will ever be fit for any service, and therefore beg leave to discharge him, and deliver him to his friends, who are willing to take care of him—McClausland is notwithstanding his rupture probably capable of some less active service...I will thank you to inform me what will be done with him.*

Lieutenant Samuel Hairston Jr., who had joined the army at the same time as Walter Coles, was in poor health in the summer of 1813 and wrote the following to General Boyd, dated August 4, 1813, from Fort George, Upper Canada: "Sir, On account of bad health, and my constitution not being able to undergo the hardships of a military life, am forced to quit the army. You will therefore please to except [*sic*] this as my resignation." However, upon being informed that the general was not "empowered to accept," he wrote to the "Honorable John Armstrong, Secy [of] War," explaining his situation: "My delicate constitution, and bad health, make me anxious to quit a service, in which I am thereby render'd almost useless. I therefore take the liberty of tendering immediately…the resignation of my commission of second Lieutenant in the United States army."

Hairston's situation was probably duplicated for many others. The hardships of a war zone, especially the intense conflicts along the Niagara frontier, were made more difficult when accompanied by sickness, a constant problem in those environments.

Letter of Second Lieutenant Samuel Hairston Jr. from Fort George Upper Canada resigning from the U.S. Army 20th Infantry Regiment. *Letters Received by the Adjutant General's Office, Record Group 94, National Archives and Records Administration, Stuart Butler.*

For the militia, those stationed in and around Norfolk were especially vulnerable. In *Defending the Old Dominion*, Stuart Butler commented that Norfolk and Hampton were well known for diseases such as malaria due to the "low lying marshes and swampy terrain." Butler quoted Congressman John Randolph in a letter to Josiah Quincy of Massachusetts in June 1813, stating that "a stranger who would go to Norfolk at this season would be reckoned a mad, and certainly a dead man." In another letter to Quincy, he noted, "Distress and alarm from the people do not arise from fear of the prowess of the enemy, but of the effects of the climate and water of the lower country."

Francis Preston, a regimental commander at Norfolk, wrote to Governor Barbour that the militia considered it a "source of alarm and a source of uneasiness to them that their destination might be to Norfolk." Militia dreaded to be called there during the summer months. But as Butler wrote, "Sickness and disease were such an undeniable fact of life in camp that they could not ignore."

This is evident by a letter found in the *Calendar of Virginia Papers*, volume 10, where on September 24, 1812, from Fort Norfolk, surgeon D.L. Claiborne of the 4th Virginia Militia Regiment informed the governor of "the prevalence of bilious [probably typhoid] fever in the Bedford Artillery Company—Twenty-six cases and two deaths. Petitioning for removal to the upper country until cool weather." Pittsylvania County shares its northern border with Bedford County.

Records show that several men from Pittsylvania County became sick around Norfolk during the war, but doubtless there were more. The following inscription was written by Martha Butcher about her husband, James Butcher, whom she married in January 1796 in Pittsylvania County:

> *James Butcher left home the 6th of June 1814 and went into the army. Was marched to Norfolk in Virginia where he was stationed. He was taken sick the 1st day of August. He got his discharge the 8th day of September and next day started home. Came by water to Petersburg, Va. here on the 16th day of September 1814 he departed this life where we hope his troubles ended.*

Drury Gammon, one of four brothers (the others being James, William and Presley) who served in the War of 1812, was a private in Captain Dr. C. Williams's company of Pittsylvania County Militia. He had married Nancy J. Smith in the county in 1804. According to her application for a widow's pension, Drury was discharged due to sickness at or near Norfolk, having served for only a short time, from June 6 to June 29, 1814. Captain Williams also had to relinquish command, for he, too, was taken sick at one time there.

Solomon Hall volunteered in Pittsylvania County, Virginia, on or about August 20, 1814, for the term of six months, but after four months, he was honorably discharged at Fort Norfolk, Virginia, "on account of sickness" on December 6, 1814. He was a member of the 7th Regiment of Virginia Militia, a private in the company of Captain Samuel Carter of Pittsylvania County. At the time he provided this information, he was laying claim to bounty land awarded for service. He died in Roane County, Tennessee.

The numbers here make it likely that Pittsylvania men were among those on the list. Stuart Butler noted in his *Defending the Old Dominion* that many sick were discharged at Norfolk. Of 1,600 regular army assigned to Norfolk in November 1814, 250 were listed as sick, with 21 deaths. Of the 4,500 militia there, 2,000 had been listed as sick, with 100 deaths. Of the 691 militia discharged that November, 290 were sick. The lack of blankets and heavy clothing for winter contributed a great deal to the sickness of the troops.

Dr. John Barraud concluded that it was more than the environment. He believed that many died due to "the effects of the militia system, bad discipline, bad cloaking, bad tents, bad cooking, all the bad consequences of bad officers and the incorrigible evils of the system."

The conditions under which the militia found themselves also contributed significantly to the discipline problem. Confronted with sickness, disease and unfamiliar surroundings, in the company of other men they did not know, in a community teeming with vices, the men did not always live up to expectations. On April 24, 1813, Brigadier General Robert Taylor, sensitive to these militia issues, wrote a somewhat optimistic note to Governor Barbour:

The progress of discipline has surpassed my expectation. Ours is not a system of terror; every means is taken to cultivate the confidence and affection of the soldiers, and to evince a proper regard for their comfort. It is however, distinctly understood that there exists the power and determination to enforce duty. Hence obedience and attention to duty are becoming matters of pride with the soldiers.

General Taylor's encouraging words notwithstanding, the militia were not normally used to strict discipline. They normally mustered twice a year in their locality to practice a few hours, a time that also included a good deal of socializing. None of this prepared them for what was expected of them. Arriving at encampments around Norfolk exposed men to, among other things already mentioned, temptations to gamble, drink and a great deal of boredom. Most of their time was spent doing routine chores about camp, but idle time and discontent created serious problems.

An indication of the temperamental nature of the militia is found in the court records of Pittsylvania County for April 1812. Thomas H. Wooding, a regimental commander and also a gentleman justice of the peace for the court, presided over a controversial situation involving a militia company. The record reads:

> *It is ordered to be certified to the executive that William S. Clark made application to this court for a recommendation as a Captain of a Volunteer company of light infantry in the second Battalion of the 101ˢᵗ regiment of the militia—and to show the propriety of his application adduced testimony to prove that William Payne, who was at the last court recommended as captain of the said company and commissioned in pursuance of the same (and the company refusing to muster under him as their Captain) declared to them that if they were not willing be commanded by him as captain, he was willing for them to choose any other person.*

It was further recorded that Payne wanted to keep his rank regardless "as appears by his certificate this day recorded," and "whereupon the vote of the company being taken, a majority was in favor of William S. Clark, and the other candidate having declined…the whole of the Company thereupon enlisted under the said William S. Clark as their Captain."

More serious issues developed in those camps around Norfolk. There were court-martials for such things as drunkenness, insubordination, gambling, sleeping on duty, stealing, failure to obey commands and fighting. The *Orderly Book of Virginia Militia* records the proceedings of a Regimental Court-Martial held on May 24, 1813, at Fort Barber for a private who "was found drunk, and too much intoxicated to perform the said piquet duty for which he had been detailed." He was sentenced to be reprimanded at the head of his company and lose his whiskey rations for ten days.

Misbehavior was so common that on May 28, 1813, Lieutenant Colonel Thomas Reade at Fort Barber issued the following regimental order to all artillery companies: "No man shall be out of camp after Tattoo. It is of the first importance that immorality of every kind particularly that of profane swearing should be suppressed in our Army, tis' highly unbecoming to the Gentlemen and the soldier."

Of course, that order did not stop "immorality of every kind." In another instance at Norfolk, on May 14, 1814, four men of the 4th Regiment were charged with playing cards (gambling). They had to ask pardon from their officers that evening, and whiskey rations were withheld for four days.

Five days later, on May 19, 1814, a captain in the 4th Regiment was court-martialed for allowing his brother in the same company to "retail spiritous liquors" to other soldiers for cash or credit. Another captain of the 5th Regiment allowed his hut to be crowded with privates, fiddling and dancing on Sunday night, and the captain was charged with "[it] being Sunday was there and extremely intoxicated." Needless to say, he was suspended from command.

At a court-martial on September 18, 1814, a private in the 6th Regiment was "sentenced to ride a wooden horse from the left to the right of the regiment" for sleeping on duty. Six days later, for the same offense, another private was punished with sweeping out the camp, being chained and confined in the guard tent and being fed bread and water.

Desertion was also a problem in the militia. One deserter was to be "confined in the black hole every night" and have "Deserter" written on the back of his coat in red letters. On June 4, 1813, a court-martial was held regarding some in Captain Samuel Calland's artillery company from Pittsylvania County. Luke Matthews was found guilty of desertion and sentenced to be "marched in front to the Regiment to which he belongs, with a label back and breast *Deserted* and be publicly reprimanded at the head of the Regiment." Three others in Calland's company—namely Benjamin B. Vicey (name partially illegible), Will Fernly (name partially illegible) and Jesse Warren—were convicted of the same charge.

Desertion was not uncommon in the army either. While not exactly desertion, the following incident shows that the army took seriously the failure to perform an assigned duty. On August 12, 1813, a U.S. infantry private listed in *William Bollings' Orderly Book* was convicted of leaving his post and leaving his gun sticking in the ground. He got eight days of hard labor.

As the war continued into 1814 and the situation became more desperate, more and more desertions took place in the army. In "Unfortunate Events" in the October 22, 2012 edition of the *New Yorker*, author Caleb Crain pointed out that the "Army shot a hundred and forty-six deserters [in 1814], up from thirty-two the year before."

Excerpt from court-martial records of men in Captain Samuel Calland's artillery company. *From* Orderly Books of the Virginia Militia 1813–1814, *vol. 1, Small Special Collections Library, University of Virginia.*

In the 3rd Regiment of Riflemen, which was recruited from Virginia, North Carolina and Tennessee and in which Captain Walter Coles of Pittsylvania County commanded his company, a list of thirty-four deserters from the Army of the United States was published on February 10, 1815, in the *Raleigh Minerva*. The sum of fifty dollars was offered for their apprehension. Most had deserted in various places and at various months in North Carolina in 1814. Corporal Hardy D. Davis, born in Wake County, North Carolina, deserted in Pittsylvania County. He was described as "aged 23 years, five feet ten and a half inches high, fair complexion, grey eyes, dark hair and by occupation a saddler, of [illegible] figure, genteel appearance, quick in spleen, large black whiskers, addicted to gambling and remarkable in cunning and villainy—deserted from Camp near Danville, Va 26th Nov. 1814."

There is no indication whether Captain Coles was acquainted with this soldier or not or whether the soldier remained in the Danville area, which was a part of the county at that time. None of the other deserters was from Captain Coles's company.

When W.J. Gordon, acting adjutant of the 3rd Rifle Regiment, published this list of these U.S. Army deserters, he closed his order by stating, "It is trusted that the good citizens of the United States will not refuse their exertions in attempting to apprehend these deluded and abandoned soldiers, who, at a period like the present day, have the folly and the meanness to desert the standard of their country."

Sad to say, Pittsylvania County soldiers in other U.S. Army units did desert. John Doudle was listed as a twenty-six-year-old farmer who enlisted in the 20th Infantry in November 1812 but deserted at Craney Island in July 1815. Also, Samuel McCulley—a twenty-one-year-old, six-foot, blue-eyed blacksmith—enlisted in Danville on August 1814 in the 20th U.S. Infantry and deserted at Fort Powhatan on New Year's Day 1816.

In one instance when Walter Coles was lieutenant in the 2nd Light Dragoons, he wrote about a deserter from his barracks at Derby, Vermont. His letter to his sister, Catherine, on April 27, 1813, reveals the drama behind searching for the soldier:

Some time since a man deserted with his horse and equipment and went into Canada, it was not known to me until ten hours had elapsed. I heard of him about two miles from the line [Canadian border] *and immediately took thirty men with me and marched to the line where I learnt that the militia were in arms to the number of one hundred for his protection. I therefore returned and began to prepare for our attack which was* [expected?] *from them. This matter however has blown over and I have been able to accomplish my purpose by dashing into the province a few miles where I was informed this deserter had first come from the interior—we took him & I have sent him for Trial to Burlington, my headquarters.*

In a letter to Captain Walter Coles in January 1815, First Lieutenant John Key of the 12th Infantry indicated that "Captain Martin of your Regiment who is now in this place [Arlington, Washington City] with 1022 of the finest men I have ever seen enlisted, they will march in the course of two days for the Regiment and of course will be with you ere long, for he has one of your deserters taken in Tennessee."

Coles had been mostly recruiting since the demise of the northern campaign with General Hampton. With desertions such as they were, and with the army never up to the designated amount authorized by Congress in January 1812, recruiting was a constant need. In another letter home, he announced that he would shortly leave Danville, Vermont, for Derby, which was about one hundred miles east of Lake Champlain and near the Canadian border. The reason was that "there are some hundred militia stationed there and being sick of infantry service, it is thought we might enlist from them a Troop."

He was in Pittsylvania County in January and February 1814, on leave from General Hampton's army. While there, he suggested that "on account of my former residence and acquaintance in the county of Pittsylvania my exertions here, in the recruiting service would probably be crowned with unusual success."

Not only was he assigned to recruit in the county, but also other records show him recruiting in Virginia from April 30 to December 14, 1814, including in Bath (County) Court House and Woodstock, Virginia. In fact, he was appointed superintendent of recruiting for the 3rd Rifle Regiment in the state.

Letter dated February 28, 1814, from Walter Coles I of Pittsylvania County on furlough from General Wade Hampton's army division. *Letters Received by the Adjutant General's Office, Record Group 94, National Archives and Records Administration, Stuart Butler.*

He must have been stationed in or near Washington, for his cousin Edward Coles wrote to "Cap. Coles of 3rd Rifle Regiment" with the invitation, "Mr. & Mrs. Madison have requested me to invite you & Carrington to dine with us today in a family way at 3 o'clock…. We see as little of you and Carrington as we shd do if you were stationed half way between this & Baltimore."

While dining with the president may have been one of the perks of being a cousin of Dolley Madison, Coles and other officers spent most of their days involved in the routine business of camp life, court-martials for disciplinary measures and recruiting to replace deserters and to add to the ranks when men were discharged sick and when enlistments were up.

While most of the Virginia Militia and soldiers of the army did not fight in a battle, they endured their time away from home bravely, honorably serving their country. They bore sickness and disease, endured hardship and stayed true to the cause in unwelcome circumstances. Had it not been for those men standing tall, it is likely this country would not be standing at all.

Chapter 8

THE EMPIRE STRIKES BACK

*We should have to fight hereafter, not for "free trade and sailors' rights," not for
the conquest of the Canadas, but for our national existence.*
—*U.S. Army captain Joseph Nicholson, after Britain's defeat of Napoleon, 1814*

During the ongoing American failures in the Canadian campaigns, and
after the Battle of Craney Island and the British attack on Hampton,
the Chesapeake Bay area remained on heightened alert. Residents faced
the possibility of renewed attacks at Norfolk and Hampton and perhaps
an attempt on Richmond by the British, who continued marauding up and
down coastal regions along the bay while maintaining their blockade.

Richmond was spared, and by the late fall of 1813, the British presence
was dramatically reduced, as much of the British squadron sailed for Halifax
and Bermuda for repairs and resupply. Still, their presence in the bay left
little doubt that they were not departing permanently.

Compounded with anxiety about British forces remaining in the bay was
the defeat of Napoleon by Britain and its allies at the Battle of Leipzig,
which was followed by Napoleon's abdication. Britain's war with France was
over, so the opportunity then existed for Britain to send thousands more
troops to America to reinforce its efforts in Canada and the Chesapeake.

While Britain was celebrating its defeat of the French dictator, its
squadrons returned to the Chesapeake Bay in force. Consequently,
militia by the thousands were called up from all over Virginia to reinforce
Norfolk and Richmond. By October 16, 1814, nearly eleven thousand

troops were encamped around Richmond and eight thousand around Norfolk. The naval base at Norfolk and the capital at Richmond were both seen as probable British objectives. But while British intentions were questionable, attacks on Washington or Baltimore were not being discounted.

Several companies commanded by Pittsylvanians served in the Norfolk area during 1814. Their deployment consisted of several weeks to months, with some lasting into February 1815:

➤ Captains William Linn, Nathaniel Wilson and Thomas Clark of Pittsylvania County commanded companies in the 7th Virginia Militia.

➤ Lieutenant James Nance's company of Pittsylvania militia served with the 4th Regiment (January 1814). The regiment was later commanded by Lieutenant Colonel Thomas Wooding of Pittsylvania County (September 1814–March 1815). Captain Thomas Ragsdale of Pittsylvania County also commanded a volunteer infantry company in the 5th Regiment (January–April 1814).

➤ The 6th Virginia Militia Regiment, commanded by Lieutenant Colonel Daniel Coleman of Pittsylvania County, had companies under Lieutenant William Lewis, Captain William Payne and Captain Dr. C. Williams, all of Pittsylvania County.

➤ Captain James Lanier's troop of cavalry served in Sales Battalion (April–May 1814).

Among those in the ranks from Pittsylvania County—both U.S. Army soldiers and Virginia Militia—who were eventually discharged from the Norfolk area was the previously mentioned Edmund Gross at Craney Island, in December 1814. Thomas Sparks in Captain William Linn's company of the 7th Virginia Regiment was mustered into service about August 1814 for six months and was discharged at Fort Barbour at Norfolk, Virginia, on February 1815.

Thomas Stewart served in Captain Nathaniel Wilson's company of light infantry in the 7th Militia Regiment for six months, enrolling in August 1814, and being discharged in February 1815; Solomon Hall, a private in the 7th Virginia Militia in the company of Captain Samuel Carter, volunteered in Pittsylvania County in late August 1814 for six months and was discharged at Norfolk in early December 1814.

Others with U.S. Army units included William Wooten, who was still present in Norfolk the last of April 1815. In March 1815, Pittsylvania

County men Joseph Berry, Micaja Boise, John Hankins, John Hissam and Thomas King were all discharged at Norfolk. William Snipes was discharged at Norfolk in July 1815.

Each of those mentioned, and others from the county as well, hovered in the forts and camps around Norfolk in 1814 in preparation for a British attack. With Richmond also threatened, other Pittsylvanians were in camps there beginning in September. Stuart Butler noted that those units ordered to Richmond were to gather at Camp Fairfield east of the city, where five new militia brigades were formed.

Among the Pittsylvania companies in the Richmond brigades were Captain Edward Carter's troop of cavalry in the 1st Virginia Cavalry. Serving in his company were his three brothers: Sergeant Rawley W. Carter, Sergeant Christopher L. Carter and Private Jesse Carter, all of Pittsylvania County. Also in the same 2nd Brigade, commanded by Brigadier General Joel Leftwich, was Captain George Townes's artillery company in the 3rd Regiment; in the 4th Regiment, both Captain Nathaniel Terry and Lieutenant John Adams commanded companies.

Captain Tunstall Shelton's company served in the 2nd D'Elite Corps at Charles City and New Kent Courthouse. In the 3rd Brigade, commanded by Brigadier General James Breckinridge, Lieutenant Colonel Daniel Coleman commanded the 6th Regiment from August to November 1814. For the most part, all these commands in the Richmond brigades ended in December 1814, when British threats appeared over. However, a British presence remained in the bay among its tributaries and inlets until the end of the war.

But it wasn't just the Chesapeake Bay region that was threatened. The entire Atlantic coast, including New England, withered under the British blockade. J.T. Headley, in *The Second War with England*, wrote, "The notes of alarm and preparation rang along coasts from Maine to Louisiana…before the mysterious shadow of the gigantic coming evil."

The addition of more European war veterans prompted the British to initiate a three-part counteroffensive against the United States that included invading the United States down Lake Champlain, attacking up the Chesapeake at Washington and especially Baltimore and attacking New Orleans to get control of the Mississippi River.

By the middle of August, Admiral Cochrane, a new commander of the British North American Station at Halifax, and British general Robert Ross had reentered the bay with twenty warships and transports filled with 4,500 veterans from the campaign against Napoleon.

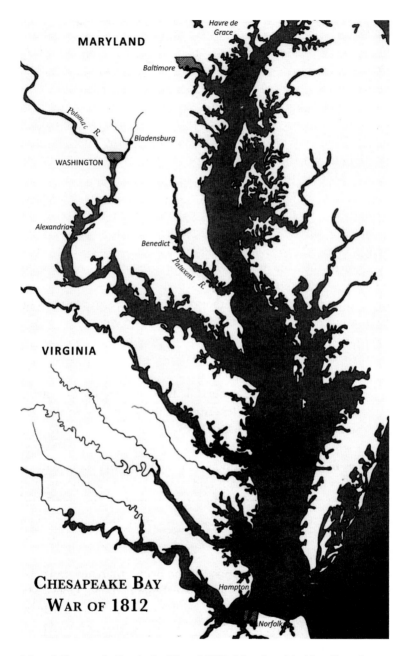

Map of Chesapeake Bay in the War of 1812. *Map after original from Center for Military History U.S. Army.*

The British sailed up the Patuxent and Potomac Rivers, threatening both Washington and Baltimore. Donald Hickey, in *The War of 1812: A Short History*, noted that Washington and Baltimore were "inviting targets." Furthermore, "a successful attack on the nation's capital would be a great blow to American pride." Baltimore was even more important because it was a major port and a center of privateering. The British wanted to put an end to this "den of pirates" (privateers) that had continually harassed His Majesty's merchant ships. Attacking both these cities would also create a diversion from the Canadian frontier.

However, the American government did not consider a British threat to Washington realistic, as it was not of strategic importance. It was little more than a small village with government buildings. Baltimore was the more likely target. Consequently, when British troops debarked at Benedict, Maryland, below Washington on August 19, no resistance to the landing was offered by American forces.

Only too late was it realized that Washington City was the objective. Upstream along the Patuxent, two dozen gunboats, commanded by American commodore Joshua Barney, had been bottled up by British warships and were destroyed by Barney's men as they raced toward Washington to stall the British advance on the capital.

On August 24, the British arrived at Bladensburg on the east branch of the Potomac, about five miles from Washington. There they engaged several thousand militia in what became known as the Bladensburg Races. Despite outnumbering the enemy forces, the hastily prepared defense by ill-trained militiamen fell apart. The men panicked in the face of Congreve rockets, and with British bayonets gleaming in the summer sun, they feared being surrounded by a circle of steel. Dropping their weapons, the Americans ran before the advancing columns of British regulars. The militia stampede left an open road all the way to Washington.

Washington was nearly abandoned as the British marched down its streets later that evening. The president and the cabinet had fled. Dolley Madison, though hearing the thunder of cannons at Bladensburg, stayed behind in the President's House, leaving only at the last minute. As she left, she saw to it that Gilbert Stuart's portrait of Washington and a copy of the Declaration of Independence were not left behind.

The British entered the abandoned President's House (now the White House) and found a dinner all prepared for a reception for forty people scheduled for that evening. After feasting on the meal and looting the mansion, the British piled furniture and other furnishings in heaps and set the mansion on fire.

Over two days, the British also burned the Capitol Building, which lodged the House of Representatives and Senate, as well as buildings comprising the Treasury, War, State and Navy Departments and the arsenal. Americans themselves destroyed the Washington Navy Yard and two unfinished vessels to prevent their capture.

It was two days of terror for those remaining in Washington, in shock as the United States capital went up in flames so bright that men could recognize one another's faces during the darkness. The gigantic flames devouring Washington City could be seen all the way from Baltimore, forty miles away. Congressional papers, the Library of Congress—all were lost. That is, all except the Patent Building.

After a severe thunderstorm, the British left in the early morning hours of August 26, leaving much of the capital a smoldering ruin. Alexandria, south of Washington, easily surrendered to British ships, which emptied its warehouses, but the British did not burn the city.

Many British considered the burning of Washington as payback for the American desecration of the Canadian capital of York, where the

Burning of Washington August 24, 1814 by the British. From engraving in The Second War with England *by J. T. Headley, 1853.*

Parliament buildings and government papers were destroyed. Yet the destruction of Washington brought outrage from the American people and helped unite the country even more, despite opposition to the war. Elbridge Gerry Jr. wrote on September 4 to his cousin Catherine Coles in Pittsylvania County about Washington and Alexandria and the fear that Boston would be also in danger:

> *I daily bring to mind the quiet retreat that protects you, and think how remote from danger our family would be in Pits* [Pittsylvania]. *I think the situation of that part of the country is very favorable unless the slaves should prove turbulent & there is no fear from that source.*
>
> *The unhappy capture of the Capital roused the people of this quarter from slumber, but could persuade only a part that danger was to be apprehended. When news of the treatment received in Alexandria reached them, a sense of danger convinced every person of the necessity of united defence, and since that period exertion has been made on all sides. Companies are forming by individuals exempt from military duty, & I am myself forming a rifle corps of true republican Americans.*

After Washington, few doubted that Baltimore, America's third-largest city after New York and Philadelphia, would be spared. But although Washington's defenses were a sad story, Baltimore would be different.

In the northern theater of war, at the same time Washington and Baltimore were being threatened, British forces numbering almost eleven thousand under Canadian general Prevost invaded the United States to split New England from the rest of the country and capture the military installation at Plattsburg, New York, on the shore of Lake Champlain. Both countries had been building ships on the lake, and the British felt they had a superior fleet.

On September 11, 1814, Prevost planned for his attack on the smaller American force at Plattsburg, commanded by General Alexander Macomb, while simultaneously attacking the American fleet on the lake with a British naval force under Captain George Downie. This would prevent the guns of the American ships from offering help to the land forces under Macomb.

The American navy in the bay under Lieutenant Thomas Macdonough was smaller than the sixteen armed vessels the British possessed, plus the British had more cannons with longer ranges than the Americans. However, the British remained at anchor in Plattsburg Bay, which gave the American fleet an advantage. When Macdonough's ships had one side battered and damaged, he used his anchors to turn the ship to the other side and use those cannons to outgun the British ships, which were not able to do the same. The British ships were disabled, and all of them surrendered. Without naval support for his troops, Prevost withdrew his invasion plans.

Almost to the day, another American victory was in the making at Baltimore. General Ross's troops, fresh from burning Washington, landed at North Point, twelve miles south of Baltimore, on September 12, 1814. They met stiff resistance from 3,500 militia, and this delayed their advance and also led to the death of General Ross. The next day, the British continued marching toward Baltimore, where the whole city had been involved in building fortifications. When the British arrived just outside the city, their forces were blocked by ten thousand militia, artillery and cavalry.

The British regulars, already dispirited by the death of General Ross, waited for their naval forces under Admirals Cochrane and Cockburn to penetrate Baltimore's harbor defenses and silence the guns of Fort McHenry, a star-shaped fortress that guarded the harbor. The British anchored bomb ships and rocket ships in a semicircle two and a half miles from the fort on the Patapsco River, out of range of McHenry's guns. If their attack on the fort was successful, other, lighter ships could move into the shallower waters of the harbor and train their guns on the American troops blocking the British land forces.

Bombardment of Fort McHenry September 13–14, 1814 during the War of 1812. From engraving in The Naval Temple *by Barber Badger, 1816.*

On the night of September 13, the citizens of Baltimore eyed the macabre fireworks display of two-hundred-pound bombs exploding, winced at the terrorizing *hiss* of Congreve rockets and their glaring light as they flew over the fort and felt the earth-shaking boom of cannons. During the night, the rain fell in downpours, with lightning intermixing with the exploding shells and fiery rockets. The bombardment continued for a full twenty-five hours from ships with names such as *Volcano, Meteor, Terror* and *Devastation.*

Eight miles away, Francis Scott Key, a Georgetown lawyer who had sought the release of a friend from a prison ship, was detained by the British until the battle was over. Even with an overcast and rainy sky, Key could see the red glow in the night that led him to write later that the "rockets' red glare, the bombs bursting in air, gave proof through the night that our flag was still there."

As day dawned the next morning, Key could then see a much larger flag than the storm flag that had flown through the night. Major Armistead, the fort's commander, had previously ordered a "flag so large that the British will have no difficulty in seeing it from a distance." The British saw the flag, too, and the bombardment ceased, as they realized that their task of reducing the fort was hopeless. So overcome with excitement was Key at seeing the huge flag, indicating that the fort had not surrendered, that he wrote the poem containing those famous words about the bombardment. "The Star-Spangled Banner" later became our national anthem. By special order of the president of the United States, a "Star-Spangled Banner" flag now flies over Fort McHenry twenty-four hours a day, seven days a week.

With the failure of the British fleet to subdue Fort McHenry, the British land forces boarded their barges and headed back to their ships, and Cochrane's forces withdrew down the bay. It was a great day for the fledging American nation; it had stood up against the British empire's enormous firepower and won. Despite the eight hundred rockets and two thousand shells fired at Fort McHenry, the Americans lost only four men killed and twenty-four wounded.

After the Battle of Fort McHenry, Catherine Coles at the family home at Coles Hill opened another letter from her cousin Elbridge Gerry Jr. of Boston, dated September 25. He remarked that "I had hardly finished reading your letter of the 5th in our exchange building, when I was interrupted by repeated cheers for news from Baltimore." But fear was in the air that Boston might be attacked next. Gerry continued, "Boston is fortifying & all things moved out, & I trust will be able to repel any attack."

The "Star-Spangled Banner" flag with its fifteen stars and fifteen stripes. Flown in Pittsylvania County at the Calland's Potpourri Festival in October 1812 in honor of the 200th anniversary of the War of 1812. *Author's collection.*

The British did not completely leave the Chesapeake Bay but continued their depredations. In October 1814, the 2nd Virginia Militia Brigade, under Brigadier General Joel Leftwich, and the 3rd Brigade, under Brigadier General James Breckinridge, were both rerouted to the Washington and Baltimore area from their camps near Richmond. They arrived at Ellicott's Mill and nearby Camp Crossroads in Maryland, both near Baltimore, in October and November, respectively.

William Gammon was one of four brothers from Pittsylvania County who served in the War of 1812 in Lieutenant John Adams's company in the 2nd Brigade under General Leftwich. Gammon had enrolled at Beavers' tavern in Pittsylvania County in August 1814. Records show that they marched to Richmond and then— by way of Fredericksburg, Dumfries, Alexandria, Georgetown, Washington City, Bladensburg and the Patuxent—to Ellicott's Mill, Maryland, where he was discharged on December 1, 1814.

William's brother Presley Gammon also served in John Adams's company at the same time. Another brother, James Gammon, was drafted in August 1814 and marched to Richmond, then Washington and then to Ellicott's Mill, where he was discharged. All the brothers, including Drury Gammon (previously mentioned as being discharged at Norfolk due to sickness), were enlisted during the summer of 1814.

While soldiers like William Gammon, his brother Presley and others from Pittsylvania County did not serve in Baltimore's militia defense during the British attack on Fort McHenry, they did continue with their units during the months following the Baltimore campaign. The immediate threat to Washington and Baltimore had dissipated, but great concern still existed about future British plans. Those suspicions were realized as Northern Neck counties continued to be looted, burned or subjected to wanton destruction.

As Stuart Butler mentioned, "With additional manpower, British ships and barges harassed and invaded the Northern Neck with impunity." With the lightning-fast British raids, Virginia militiamen were unable to reach

Pay roll for William Gammon of Pittsylvania County, dated December 12, 1814, Baltimore. *National Archives and Records Administration, Pension Files for War of 1812, Chris Hanks.*

Discharge certificate for William Gammon of the Pittsylvania Militia, Lieutenant John Adams's company. *National Archives and Records Administration, Pension Files for War of 1812, Chris Hanks.*

those locations before the British had left the scene. Butler concluded that Northern Neck counties "suffered the most economic damage from British attacks than any part of Virginia."

During this time, a letter from Daniel Coleman of Pittsylvania County, who commanded the 6th Regiment, was addressed to Brigadier General James Breckinridge, commandant of the 3rd Brigade, Brigade Quarters, Camp Mitchell, near Richmond. It shows the extent to which the Virginia Militia continued to defend against British atrocities in the Northern Neck after the British left Baltimore but also illustrates the type of depredations carried on by the British during their blockade of the bay.

In the letter, Coleman related his troop movements from Tappahannock, Virginia, into Virginia's Northern Neck and his attempts to confront the British at St. George Island, Richmond (County) Court House, Monday's Point, Northumberland Court House, Cone River and Middle Creek. However rapidly he marched his men to those sites, in each case the British had returned to their ships ahead of the militia.

He recounted one instance when the British had taken a Dr. Jones prisoner and "were pillaging the country in that vicinity." In another instance, he related how "the enemy, amounting to 100, were on shore, near the mouth of Cone River, shooting stock on the plantation of Doctor Ball."

Coleman also described how his troops had joined Colonel Thomas Downing's regiment near Northumberland Court House after Downing's skirmish with the British and noted the losses on both sides. He then informed General Breckinridge that he was taking his command to Lancaster County, Virginia, to join the forces with Colonel John Chewning.

The continued defense of Virginia by the militia did not receive the national attention that the victories at Lake Champlain and the defense of Baltimore did. But while those great victories inspired the nation, an even greater victory was coming at New Orleans, the key to the Mississippi and Louisiana Territory.

Before the battle at New Orleans, Creek Indian uprisings in the South had led to attacks on forts and farms in Georgia and Alabama. In August 1813, a band of about four thousand Creeks called Red Sticks conducted a most horrendous attack on Fort Mims outside Mobile. The Creeks massacred or burned most of the inhabitants, including women and children, and took 250 scalps. In consequence, the southern states of Georgia, Tennessee and Mississippi Territory called out the militias.

General Andrew Jackson of Tennessee, with 2,500 men, marched into Creek territory. Among those who served with Andrew Jackson in the

TRANSCRIPT OF LETTER FROM DANIEL COLEMAN TO GENERAL JAMES BRECKINRIDGE

Camp Farnham Church, Richmond Cty October 8th 1814

Sir

The attachment under my command arrived at Tappahannock on Monday morning the 3rd of Oct, & being much delayed in crossing the river, did not all get over until Tuesday evening, a little before sunset. On reaching the shore, in the Northern neck, I received a dispatch from Major Tuberville, requesting the aid of Captain Lyle's Troop to repel the Enemy, who had landed opposite to St. George Island, taken Dr. Jones prisoner and were pillaging the country in that vicinity. I ordered Captain Lyle and troop to proceed that night by a forced march to the place of danger, but unfortunately, before their arrival, the enemy had taken to his Barges, & the troops were disappointed. In the meantime I proceeded with all possible rapidity by way of Richmond C'House toward the point assailed, but being there informed that a party of the enemy had landed at a place called Monday's point, another about six miles of this place & directed my course thitherwards, continuing my march nearly all night with a view to make an attack on him in the Morning; but on arriving here, I learned that he has left the former place, concentrated his forces and taken possession of Northumberland C'House.

I therefore took the road leading to the C'House and within seven miles of that place joined Col. Downing, who had collected the skeleton of a Regiment, amounting to something like a hundred men who had been skirmishing with the enemy the greater part of Tuesday the 4th Inst—No injuries on our part was sustained, except the loss of four or five men taken prisoners, and the capture of the ammunition wagon belonging to the Infantry—The loss of the enemy was the capt of their Bomb ship and one private killed and four privates taken prisoners.

After affecting a junction with Downing's party, we continued our march to within four miles of the N C'House, when on Wednesday evening we ascertained that the enemy had embarked in his Barges, we therefore discontinued our march & encamped for the night. On the morning of the next day, receiving intelligence that a party of the enemy, amounting to 100, were on shore, near the mouth of Cone River, shooting stock on the plantation of Doctor Ball. I resolved to go thither and make an effort to cut him off, but in arriving there in the evening, was informed that he had taken to his vessels about 10 o'clock on the morning of that day. I then took up the line of march for this place, with a view to return to Brigade Quarters, being well convinced that the enemy had deserted the Potomac. But understanding this morning by an express from Colo Downing of Lancaster, that 22 of the enemy's ships had anchored near the mouth of Middle Creek, in that county, and that 5 Barges had run up that creek, with a view to plunder stock & Negroes, have decided that we will go down & try our fortune with them at that place.

This step I conceive is rather contrary to the letter of your instructions but not to the spirit. If I am wrong I hope to be excused, & ordered to take a different course. I have taken the liberty of keeping Kennedy's wagon, finding it impossible to do without it, as we have, on account of the scarcity of provisions in the Northern neck to procure provisions from the Rappahannock. The troops are in fine health and spirits with the exception of a few, who were very sick but are getting better.

I am Sir, with sentiments of high respect yr Hbl servt, Daniel Coleman, Colo Comdr of the 6ᵗʰ Regiment.

southern campaign was Dr. Thomas Fearn. He was born in Pittsylvania County and received his early schooling in Danville. After attending Washington College in Lexington, Virginia, he established a medical practice in Alabama and during the Creek War served as a regimental surgeon in the Tennessee Militia.

Jackson's forces finally defeated the Creeks soundly on March 27, 1814, at the Battle of Horseshoe Bend. About 800 Red Sticks were killed and 350 women and children taken prisoner. With the Treaty of Fort Jackson the following August, the Creek War ended with the Creeks ceding 23 million acres to the United States. Jackson's victory over the Creeks also led to his appointment as commander of all United States forces in the southern theater and set the stage for the last big battle of the War of 1812.

British admiral Cochrane, whose attack on Baltimore had failed, initiated plans for British warships and troops to be sent to the Gulf of Mexico to stage an attack on New Orleans. Donald Hickey in *The War of 1812* noted that New Orleans was "the largest city west of the Appalachian Mountains, and the principal outlet for Western commodities."

A large British force appeared off Mississippi's coast in early December 1814 and made its way by land toward New Orleans. With British reinforcements arriving under General Sir Edward Packenham, the British force totaled fourteen thousand men, three times more than American forces. But Andrew Jackson, who had cobbled together an unlikely force there, was not intimidated.

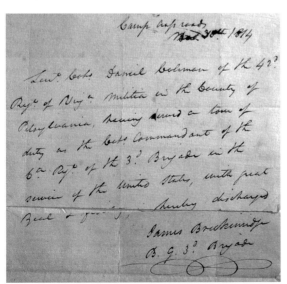

Discharge certificate of Lieutenant Colonel Daniel Coleman of the 42nd Regiment Pittsylvania County Militia, who served as a commandant of the 6th Virginia Militia Regiment in the War of 1812. Signed by Brigadier General James Breckinridge at Camp Crossroads near Baltimore, dated November 30, 1814. *National Archives and Records Administration, Pension Files for War of 1812, Chris Hanks.*

Jackson's four thousand men were a hodgepodge collection of whomever he could muster. John Grant and Ray Jones, in their book *The War of 1812*, wrote that "[a]mongst them were frontiersmen from Tennessee and Kentucky, freed black slaves and creoles, French- and Spanish-speaking planters and fishermen, Choctaw warriors, and perhaps even pirates who had served under the swashbuckling Captain Jean Lafitte."

On January 8, 1815, thousands of British soldiers, with bayonets fixed, lined up and marched across a quarter mile of open ground. It was an all-out assault on Jackson's defenses at New Orleans, which included batteries of heavy artillery. The British quickly suffered major casualties from Jackson's forces. By the battle's end, the British had lost nearly two thousand killed, wounded or captured, with Jackson losing fewer than one hundred men. A British veteran of the Napoleonic Wars in Europe described the Battle of New Orleans as "the most murderous fire I ever beheld before or since." For the British, it was the worst defeat of the war.

Andrew Jackson defeated the British in the Battle of New Orleans on January 8, 1815, after a peace treaty had been agreed to by British and American negotiators on Christmas Eve 1814. *Wikimedia Commons.*

Rachel Donelson Jackson's portrait in the Pittsylvania County Courthouse in Chatham, Virginia. She was the daughter of John Donelson, a founder of Tennessee, and also the wife of Andrew Jackson, the hero of the Battle of New Orleans and the seventh president of the United States. *Author's collection.*

Even though Washington had been left in ashes, the Atlantic coast had been successfully blockaded and the British had occupied part of New England, the Battle of New Orleans was an enduring victory for the Americans. And the citizens of New Orleans celebrated it with vigor and enthusiasm, elevating Andrew Jackson almost to sainthood over the outcome. Even Jackson's wife, Rachel, and their adopted son came to New Orleans to share in the excitement.

Rachel Jackson was born in 1767 in Pittsylvania County, Virginia, but left at age twelve when her father, John Donelson, moved his family to Tennessee and helped establish what is now Nashville. She met Andrew Jackson while he was a young lawyer staying at her mother's boardinghouse. Jackson was strong-willed in most matters and belligerent against his enemies, but Rachel was a tempering spirit. Her gentle persuasion during their marriage carried much weight with him, although he did not always follow her advice.

Rachel's simplicity and unadorned manner did not lend her an air of sophistication, especially in the elegant society of New Orleans. She nevertheless regaled in her husband's success, while looking at the culture with a jaundiced eye. She wrote then, "I have seen more already than in all my life past it is the finest Country for the Eye of a Strainger [*sic*] but a Little while he tir[e]s of the Dissipation…So much amusement balls Concerts Plays theatres &c &c but we Don't attend half of them."

After the war, when the United States acquired Spanish Florida, Jackson was appointed military governor, much against Rachel's wishes. On their trip to Florida, they first arrived at New Orleans by steamboat in April 1821. Rachel was becoming increasingly religious and was very blunt about her feelings being back in that society. She wrote, "Great Babylon is come up before me! Oh, the wickedness, the idolatry of this place! Unspeakable riches and splendor. The attention and honors paid to the General far excell the recital of my pen."

She could well do without New Orleans and longed for the simple life of their log cabin at the Hermitage just outside Nashville, Tennessee. But New Orleans had not forgotten Jackson, and its citizens reveled in his great victory that had saved the city.

Coming after the American victory at Lake Champlain in the north and the failure of the British to take Baltimore, the victory over the British at New Orleans in the south put an end to Great Britain's designs to destabilize the United States. Besides, with Jackson's victory coming two weeks after a peace treaty between the two nations had been signed, Americans believed that they had won the war.

Chapter 9
ONE NATION AFTER ALL

The war, with its vicissitudes is illustrating the capacity and the destiny of the United States to be a great, a flourishing, and a powerful nation.
—President James Madison, 1812

Peace talks between Great Britain and America began in August 1814 and continued on into December. The British were counting on victories on Lake Champlain and at Baltimore, as well as counting on the capture of New Orleans, as a means of forcing concessions from the United States during the negotiations. But their hopes were dashed, and on Christmas Eve 1814 in Belgium, the American ambassador to Russia, John Quincy Adams, as well as Americans Henry Clay and Albert Gallatin, signed their names to the Treaty of Ghent, giving America one of its best Christmas presents.

It took weeks for the treaty to arrive in Washington, and only after the Battle of New Orleans did the U.S. Senate ratify it, on February 18, 1815. The Treaty of Ghent left the United States intact, with both sides agreeing to status quo antebellum, returning to the state of things before the war. Basically, it was a truce, with neither side giving up anything. But although the treaty recognized no victor, America accomplished something remarkable in the War of 1812: it didn't lose.

It takes little imagination to see how the war could have gone the other way. America entered the war unprepared militarily, with an army that had been gutted of men and arms and a navy that had been reduced to a skeleton fleet of warships. The country was plagued with uncertain reasons for going to war and with a divided Congress that barely approved it. Political divisions almost split the country apart internally toward the end as talk of secession ran rampant in New England.

The country also suffered from incompetent military leadership in its various campaigns, vicious opposition from Indian tribes aligned with the British and a government that struggled to finance the war, essentially becoming bankrupt by the end of the conflict.

The fate of the nation came down to the last few months. By then, America's military leadership and fighting ability had shown marked improvement, but the defeat of Napoleon enabled the British to send more veteran troops and ships to prosecute the war in America.

The British had anxiously anticipated America's defeat. In early September 1814, Captain David Milne of the HMS *Bulwark*, then off the coast of New England, relished in the British blockade that had the "whole coast in continual alarm." He bragged about the British command of the Chesapeake and the burning of Washington. "A sad and despicable [*sic*] set," he called America's people, claiming that all that was needed was for England to send a large body of troops to conquer America. That was before Fort McHenry and New Orleans.

Had the British won more victories the final year, the outcome of the war might have been considerably different. The United States likely would have seen westward expansion stymied, with a resurgence of Indian warfare. The Mississippi River would have been less available as a means of trade for settlers, part of Maine that was under British occupation would have been severed from the country and access to the Great Lakes would have been severely limited. Plus, the United States quite possibly would have been forced into economic ties to Britain that would have made us more servants than sons of freedom.

But there is something to be said for standing up to a superpower nation like Great Britain and living to tell about it. So, the most important impact of the Treaty of Ghent was that the United States was not a defeated nation. In fact, Donald Hickey, quoted in the *New Yorker*, called the Treaty of Ghent America's "most significant victory." *The Encyclopedia of the War of 1812* concluded:

> *The United States of America had fought the world's mightiest empire to a standoff, which was in itself something of a victory. The larger triumph came in the clear assertion of U.S. nationality and Britain's implicit acknowledgment of complete U.S. independence through the*

Treaty of Ghent. As of 1815, for the first time in its brief existence, the American Republic was secure.

Then, too, Britain had had enough of us. The British wanted this protracted conflict over because the Napoleonic Wars in Europe had drained His Majesty's treasury, and the British people were tired of war. The economic cost in ships and men Britain committed to the war, the loss of trade with America, its own loss of property and the internal dissension within Great Britain were heavy prices to pay for insisting on its right to have its way on the high seas.

The fact that Great Britain, the mightiest empire on earth at that time, accepted the Treaty of Ghent as a stalemate, assured America that the British had learned their lesson and would no longer violate the country's neutrality. Although Britain never gave up its right to impress sailors on the high seas or to violate our neutral shipping, it never again resorted to this practice. The end of the European wars made both practices unnecessary, and neither issue was mentioned in the treaty.

Even the great prime minister Winston Churchill, in his *History of the English Speaking Peoples*, had to agree that Britain had learned its lesson. He had thought the War of 1812 was a "futile and unnecessary conflict" that had created an "evil legend that the struggle had been a second war of independence against British tyranny." However, having said that, he conceded that "the United States were never again refused proper treatment as an independent Power. The British Army and Navy had learned to respect their former colonials."

The War of 1812 was more than a lust for land by a government and a people anxious to expand across the continent. In a larger sense, it was the American Revolution, Part II. It was about true independence as a nation, as opposed to being treated as a second-class nation by the rest of the world. It was about America's sovereignty and finally being recognized as such. The bottom line is that America got what it went to war for.

However, the United States, as a new nation, was young and inexperienced. Since the war was its first declared war against another country, America certainly learned some lessons—one being how not to fight a war.

After the war, President Madison wasted no time in approving bills to authorize a better-organized and better-equipped standing army and navy, a national bank to enable the government to fund its operations and higher tariffs on imported goods to protect American industry and commerce from foreign competition. Madison also extended internal taxes that had been necessary because of the war. Each of these went against the philosophy of Jefferson's Democratic-Republicans, but the war revealed the need to be prepared militarily and economically.

Besides lessons learned, the war had its magnificent moments. New heroes emerged: James Lawrence, the dying captain of the USS *Chesapeake* who uttered the iconic words, "Don't give up the ship"; Oliver Hazard Perry, who defeated the British in the Battle of Lake Erie, announcing, "We have met the Enemy and they are ours"; and several men who went on to become president of the United States—James Monroe, John Quincy Adams, Andrew Jackson, William Henry Harrison and Zachary Taylor. There was the *Constitution* ("Old Ironsides") and "The Star-Spangled Banner" anthem, which has become America's paean of victory. And that thirty-two- by forty-foot flag that flew over Fort McHenry is preserved at the Smithsonian Institution, where it is displayed for every American to see.

Not to be ignored was Dolley Madison's effort to save the Gilbert Stuart portrait of George Washington at the President's House. Her unselfish gesture was no small act of bravery. As the British marched into Washington, she wrote to her sister, Anna Cutts, "Alas, I can descry only groups of military wandering in all directions, as if there was a lack of arms, or of spirit to fight for their own fireside!…I insist on waiting until the large picture of Gen. Washington is secured."

Dolley Madison, with her outgoing personality, enlivened the social scene at the President's House and in Washington. Her social gatherings brought together political opposites, allowing them to meet away from the hostile debates in Congress. She became her husband's political confidante and liberated the role of women in some respects by her activities. It is understandable, then, why she was the first wife of a president to be referred to as the "First Lady." Not bad for a woman with Pittsylvania County connections.

Beyond the heroes and the moments of glory, the War of 1812 was ultimately a test of resolve on whether this nation would survive or descend into second-class nationhood, a pawn in the hand of other more powerful nations. The country was sorely tested at places such as Lundy's Lane, Plattsburg, Lake Erie, Washington, Fort McHenry, New Orleans and throughout the Chesapeake. Looking back, it seems ironic that those battles were with Canada and Britain. Both are now this country's closest friends and strongest allies. In fact, the border between Canada and the United States is the longest unguarded border in the world.

Not only was the country as a whole tested, but Pittsylvania County soldiers were tested as well. Pittsylvania County men such as Captain Walter Coles and Lieutenant Samuel Hairston and a number of others served in various regiments of the U.S. Army in the contentious northern frontier. And from Pittsylvania County's 42nd and 101st Regiments, fifteen companies or detachments were called into service with the Virginia militia during the war.

Defending the citizens and land of Virginia against British invasion involved uncertain risks. It was no stroll on the beach for those who served along the waters of the Chesapeake Bay and its tributaries or for those who served along the Great Lakes. Britain's Duke of Wellington defeated Napoleon at the Battle of Waterloo, exclaiming for all time that war was "damned serious business."

The Pittsylvania militiamen who were called up did their duty, and even those companies that were not called up for service remained at readiness to serve. And that is enough. A quote attributed to Confederate general Robert E. Lee bears repeating here: "Duty is the most sublime word in our language. Do your duty in all things. You cannot do more. You should never wish to do less."

The men of Pittsylvania County who marched the long roads to Richmond and Norfolk and beyond, as well as those who found themselves in unhealthy climates and unknown circumstances far from home, were armed and ready to meet the enemy. Their attitude was perhaps reflected in the words of Lieutenant James Nance, who led a Pittsylvania County militia company. In a family register with the inscription "James

Flag of the 42nd Regiment of Pittsylvania County Militia. This is the official Pittsylvania County flag; the original is in the county courthouse in Chatham, Virginia. *Author's collection.*

Nance his book," he wrote these words: "1814 January the 4th I started to Norfolk in defence [*sic*] of my Country."

There is no indication that James Nance ever saw battle, but just the concept of "my Country" says it all. In the end, the god of battles honored Virginia's soldiers for their commitment, and with his help, the Second War of Independence guaranteed that this nation would survive and prosper. They, along with soldiers from other states, all made possible a new day for America.

The period after the war was a new beginning called the "Era of Good Feelings." A book review quote from "The Effect of War of 1812 Upon the Consolidation of the Union" states: "The bonds of the early days of the Revolution were forged anew, and the nation's heart beat as one...An era of good feelings had dawned."

Albert Gallatin, Madison's secretary of the treasury, said, "The war has renewed and reinstated the national feelings and character which the Revolution had given, and which were daily lessened...The People...are more American; they feel and act more as a nation."

This nationalism was enhanced near the end of the war, as the Federalist Party went on life support after holding a convention in Hartford, Connecticut, that simmered with talk of secession and of rewriting the Constitution to limit the powers of Congress and the president. The year 1814 had been one of other traitorous actions by New England states. Parts of Maine, which had become occupied by the British, made a separate peace with Britain and refused to pay federal taxes. Even the governor of Massachusetts declared that the state would consider defending Canada in exchange for British military assistance if the state seceded.

Those actions lost traction, especially after the victory at New Orleans and with a peace treaty that left America intact. The demise of the Federalist Party and the fractious debates that had divided the country dissipated, and national unity became the order of the day. For a time, there was a sense of oneness and harmony, as people all across the United States saw within themselves a singleness of purpose.

This unity, however, had taken a war. William Bennett wrote in *America: The Last Best Hope*, "The War of 1812 helped to form a new American consciousness. The American identity was fused in the crucible of battle." A National Park Service essay on the Star-Spangled Banner National Historic Trail concludes in a similar manner that America had come out of the war a more mature nation: "Having been tested against a world superpower, the states were now more truly 'unified'."

The war not only united the nation but also changed it internally. Bruce and William Cotton, in *Bold and Magnificent Dream*, insist that the War of 1812 was "one of America's most significant experiences…. It changed the way Americans thought about themselves."

This was quite a change, since beforehand, Americans had identified themselves more with their locality or state and had not really thought of themselves as one nation. As George Tindall stated in his *America: A Narrative History*, "Nationhood was not the dominant idea of the Revolution. Even after the initial war for independence, America's citizens identified with Europe, either adopting the political philosophy of France, or Britain, and economically, exchanging goods across the sea with European nations." The War of 1812 changed that.

Just like the Embargo of 1807, the war resulted in the coasts being blockaded and trade with other nations sharply curtailed. With imports and exports from Great Britain and other countries halted, America grew more self-reliant. For instance, the American textile industry grew exponentially from 1807 to 1815, and its growth continued afterward.

By 1820, despite the financial panic of 1819 that came from too rapid growth, the Industrial Revolution had begun to take hold, marked by increased internal improvements such as roads, canals and bridges. Factories dotted the landscape, and later, mechanized travel emerged with railroads, as steam engines came of age. By 1850, America was a major industrial power.

This economic revolution also affected Pittsylvania County. The two hat factories in the county in 1810 during Jefferson's Embargo increased to eleven by 1820. Herman Melton, in his *Picks, Tracks and Bateaux*, wrote, "The growth in the manufacture of tobacco products between 1820 and 1850 may be the most astounding story in the history of industry in Pittsylvania County. The 1820 inventory listed only two factories, but their number exploded to 42 by 1850." It was during this time that the county became the top tobacco-producing county in Virginia—and still remains so. Also, it is hard to argue against the probability that tobacco, even before the advent of Dan River Mills, "built" Pittsylvania County in the decades after the War of 1812.

The War of 1812 was also the impetus for the Monroe Doctrine. James Monroe, who followed Madison as president, announced that "[t]he American continents…are henceforth not to be considered as subject for future colonization by any European power." Empowered after establishing its sovereignty, America now felt confident enough to enforce violations of the sovereignty of other nations in its hemisphere.

It might also be said that the years following the War of 1812 opened the door to the Civil War, which forever made us a Union. Without any further interference from Great Britain on American frontiers as a consequence of the war, the population of the United States increased rapidly over the next decades. Gordon Wood proposed in *Smithsonian Magazine* that "[t]he nation's growth and inward turn deepened the divide between the agricultural slave states and the urbanizing industrializing North." New states that came into being could be slave or free, and that, in part, led to the Civil War.

A major question has always been, "Who won the war of 1812?" The Canadians have good cause to declare that they won, since they repelled every invasion attempt and developed their own sense of nationalism because of the war. The war broke the back of Indian resistance to westward expansion, so native groups obviously lost. And while it can be argued that America did not win the War of 1812, America did win the future.

Just as America was never the same after the War of 1812, neither was Pittsylvania County. After the war, the county continued its role as a conduit for westward expansion, as some families moved to other states or to lands in new territories made available by the government. And the county continued to grow until, by 1820, Pittsylvania County's population had increased another 22 percent from the 17,000 in 1810. And with its economy prospering, Pittsylvania County joined the rest of Virginia and the nation in the "Era of Good Feelings" and the Industrial Revolution.

This nation, which started on the shores of Virginia, not only has prospered beyond imagination but also has made its presence known by satellites into the far reaches of outer space, even to the edge of the solar system. To parrot the words of the world's first man on the moon, Neil Armstrong, the War of 1812 was a small war on the landscape of history but was, in many ways, a giant leap for America's future. Regardless of divisive issues that have colored America's history since then, America always has the model of unity that followed the War of 1812 as a template for success.

Ultimately, the War of 1812 was America's struggle for its place in the sun, and now, two hundred years later, the sun is still shining.

Chapter 10
A GRATEFUL NATION

The Militia of Virginia…throughout the war, upon all occasions, and under all circumstances…have served their country.
—*Virginia governor Wilson Cary Nicholas, Adjutant General's Final Order, 1815*

Two days after President Madison signed the Treaty of Ghent, the adjutant general of Virginia issued a final order to the Virginia Militia. Speaking for the governor, he congratulated the militia for its willingness to serve its country and "for the fortitude, with which they have borne every fatigue and danger, and for their valor in the field."

With the War of 1812 over, Pittsylvania County soldiers serving in the various campaign theaters—if their enlistments had not expired already—returned to their homes. Those born in Pittsylvania County/ Danville who served in the United States Army were discharged in various parts of the campaign theaters, whereas most Virginia militiamen were discharged in the Richmond and Norfolk areas, although some were discharged in and around Maryland.

The U.S. Army soldiers who enlisted in Danville or Pittsylvania County, in addition to those previously mentioned, include Giles Johnson, Bird Hardy and Alexander Watson, all of whom enlisted in 1813 and were discharged from the 10th Infantry at Pass Christian, Mississippi, in 1817. Giles Wilson, also born in the county, enlisted in Danville in the 20th Infantry in 1813 and was discharged at Fort Saint Marks, Florida, in December 1815. John Russell enlisted in Danville in the 28th

Infantry in September 1814 and was discharged at Detroit, Michigan, in February 1816.

Because the Virginia Militia units that were called up were put under the authority of the federal government, the men became eligible for bounty lands from public-owned lands out west. Soldiers were usually awarded 160 acres, which could be claimed by their widows if they were married before 1815. At first, they had to have served sixty days, but later land acts allowed a claim if the soldier served fourteen days. These bounty land certificates could also be passed on to their children. More than one land grant would be received by the same person to total 160 acres.

Lieutenant John Adams, who commanded a Pittsylvania Militia company, received a land grant in Illinois. Mary Fuller, wife of Jesse Fuller, a private in Captain Samuel Calland's company, was awarded land in Nebraska, as was Samuel Blair, who served in Captain Carter's company.

Kerenhappuck Smoot had married John Shumate in Fauquier County, Virginia, and settled in Pittsylvania County before the war. She filed for bounty land twice as the widow of John Shumate, who was a private in Captain Williams's Pittsylvania Company and had died in Maryland in 1814

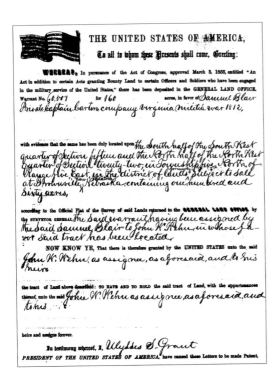

Bounty land certificate for Samuel Blair, private in Captain Carter's company, Pittsylvania Militia. *United States Department of Interior, Bureau of Land Management.*

Bounty land certificate for Mary Fuller, widow of Jesse Fuller, who served as a private in Captain Calland's company of artillery during the War of 1812. *United States Department of Interior, Bureau of Land Management.*

during the war. She also received a widow's pension of $3.50 monthly. Their son Benjamin remained in Pittsylvania County, but his brother, Samuel Shumate, migrated to Missouri.

Bounty Land Certificate No. 7,226 granted lands in Missouri to Ephraim Giles Jr., who was born in Loudon County about 1770 and moved to Pittsylvania County with his father, John Cristie Giles, in 1796. Unlike most of those veterans receiving land grants for their service in the War of 1812, Giles actually moved to Missouri with his family and died there in 1841.

Meredith Jennings, born in Pittsylvania County in 1767, became an ensign in Captain Nathaniel Terry's company. He was drafted in Pittsylvania County on or near September 1, 1814, for three months and was honorably discharged at Ellicott's Mill in Maryland. Jennings was awarded 160 acres in Missouri in 1857. In his original claim in 1856 for the bounty land, Jennings was sixty-nine years of age and had moved from Pittsylvania County to Madison, Tennessee.

William Mays, in a "Bounty Land Claim" form dated November 18, 1850, indicated that he had served in Tunstall Shelton's company of the 101st Regiment and that he was drafted at "Hames" (Haymes) in Pittsylvania

Certificate of identity and oath of service for Banister Hardy, a lieutenant in Captain John Coles's company. *National Archives and Records Administration, Chris Hanks.*

County for six months but was discharged after three months and sixteen days at Charles City Court House on December 27, 1814. In a "Claim for Minor Children for Bounty Land" in August 1890, Mays is identified by his service, and it is noted that he had died in 1876 and left "no widow surviving him." The document indicates that his child, Mary Ann Mays, for which the bounty land application was made, was fifty-two and that she was making this application based on the Act of Congress 1855.

Most veterans or their surviving widows did not settle the bounty lands they were granted but rather sold their claims to speculators instead. Bounty land certificates of Pittsylvania County men that were sold to others show the date of transaction, the acreage and location of the lands and to whom the land was sold, and it was signed "by authority of" the president of the United States at that time. That the granting and selling of bounty lands went on for decades after the war is indicated by the names of the authorizing president, including Martin Van Buren, Franklin Pierce, James Buchanan, Abraham Lincoln and Ulysses S. Grant.

Claim for minor children for bounty land for Mary Ann Mays by guardian Sally Mays. *National Archives and Records Administration, Chris Hanks.*

Besides bounty lands, pension acts were passed by Congress in 1871 and 1878 and applied to those veterans still alive or to their widows. However, by 1883, few pensioners were still alive, and widows filed pension applications on account of their husbands' services. In the 1883 list for Pittsylvania County, there are sixty-five pensioners listed. Only eight were listed as survivors of the war; the remaining fifty-seven were widows of those who had served in the War of 1812.

Among the men was Drury Mayhue, who received a pension of eight dollars per month. He was eighty-two years old in 1871, when he filed his "Declaration for Pension" application. He indicated on the form that he was drafted in August 1814 for six months as a private in Captain Jesse Leftwich's company at Haymes in Pittsylvania County and that he was discharged in December 1814 at Norfolk on account of sickness. It also stated that he had previously received two bounty land warrants for eighty acres each.

The widow pensioners of 1883 listed their post office addresses from all over the county. Among them were Berger's Store, Brosville, Callands, Chalk Level, Chatham, Chestnut Level, Malmaison, Malondsville,

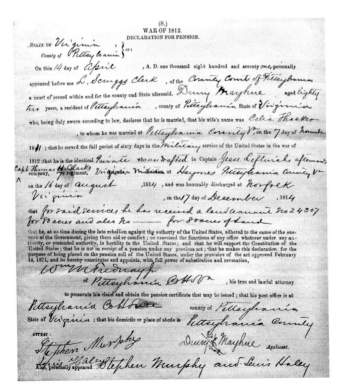

Declaration for pension from Drury Mayhew, a private in Captain Jesse Leftwich's company and, afterward, Captain Thomas H. Clark's company. *National Archives and Records Administration, Chris Hanks.*

Pleasant Gap, Peytonsburg, Riceville, Ringgold, Shockoe Church, Sycamore Station and Whitmell.

Among the widow pensioners was Martha Womack, who received an eight-dollar-per-month pension. Her "Claim for Widows Pension" application was dated April 22, 1878, and noted that she had been married to William Womack, who served in Captain Edward Carter's cavalry company. Womack was enlisted in September 1814 at Haymes, Pittsylvania, and was discharged at Richmond.

Of particular interest in the pension files was a letter written on September 25, 1878, to J.A. Bentley, Esq., decrying the delay in getting a pension for Joel Hubbard:

> *Dear Sir. I Saw Mr Joel Hubbard this morning he is the identical man you wish to know about and there is no doubt but what he served in the war of 1812 he thinks the Pension Department at washington is Very Slow in granting his certificate. Send it on as soon as you can if you please. He has worn himself out preaching he has been at it for 62 years.*
>
> *Very Respectfully,*
> *J.T. Jones,*
> *PM Riceville Pittsylvania County Va*

Benjamin W.S. Cabell, a War of 1812 soldier who came to Pittsylvania County after the war, is buried in Danville. Research by local historian Chris Hanks indicates that Cabell was enrolled at Read's Store in Campbell County in August 1814 and later attached to Captain Samuel Johnston, whose company marched to Ellicott's Mill, Maryland, near Baltimore. Cabell was discharged there that December. He married the year after the war and moved to Danville, where he remained. He continued in the militia and eventually rose to the rank of major general. He also served several terms in Virginia's General Assembly representing Pittsylvania County and was a delegate to Virginia's Constitutional Convention of 1829–30.

In the National Archives, Hanks discovered a letter written by Cabell from his home at Bridge Water in Pittsylvania County near Danville and dated November 26, 1852. It was addressed to Edward A. Cabell, the principal clerk of the land office in Washington, D.C. The seventeen-page letter lists a number of local veterans' names and details about their places of muster and service. Benjamin Cabell was assisting those veterans in obtaining the bounty lands that they were awarded for their service.

WAR OF 1812.

Claim of Widow for Pension, under the Provisions of Sections 4736 to 4740 inclusive Revised Statutes, and the Act of March 9, 1878.

State of _Virginia_ } ss.
County of _Pittsylvania_ }

On this _22_ day of _April_, A. D. one thousand eight hundred and _seventy eight_ personally appeared before me, _G & Kabell Db for Hajames in Pitts Co Ct_, the same being a **Court of Record** within and for the county and state aforesaid, (1) _Martha J Womack_ aged _73_ years, a resident of _Pittsylvania Co._ in the State of _Virginia_, who, being duly sworn according to law, declares that she is a widow of (2) _Wm. Womack_, deceased, who was the identical (3) _Wm. Womack_, who served under the name of (4) _Wm. Womack_ as a (5) _____ in the company commanded by Captain _Edward Carter_, in the regiment of _U.S. Calvary_, commanded by _Col. J. Holcombe_ in the war of 1812; that her said husband (6) _enlisted_ _Haymes, Pittsylvania_ on or about the _11°_ day of _Sept._, A. D. _1814_ for the term of _____, and continued in actual service in said war for the term of (7) _14 days or more_ and whose services terminated, by reason of (8) _an honorable discharge_ _Richmond_, on the _____ day of _____, A. D. _____. She further states that the following is a full description of her said husband at the time of his enlistment, viz: (9) _age about 20 yrs occupation, farmer, born in Pitts Co, Va; height 6 ft 2 inches hazel eyes, dark hair dark complexion_ She further states that she was married to the said _Wm. Womack_, at the city (or town) of _____, in the county of _Pittsylvania_, and in the State of _Virginia_, on the _16"_ day of _July_ A. D. _1825_, by one (10) _Wm. Blair_, who was a (11) _Baptist preacher_ and that her name before her said marriage was _Martha J Thompson_, and that she has not remarried since the death of the said soldier; and she further states that (12) _neither she nor her said husband were ever married before their said marriage on the 16 July 1825_ and that her said husband (13) _Wm. Womack_, died at _Pittsylvania Co._, in the State of _Virginia_, on the _26"_ day of _Nov 15_, A. D. _1849_, and she further declares that the following have been the places of residence of herself and her said husband since the date of his discharge from the Army, viz: (14) _Pittsylvania County, Va_

She makes this declaration for the purpose of obtaining the pension to which she may be entitled under the provisions of Sections 4736 to 4740 inclusive Revised Statutes, and the Act of March 9, 1878, and hereby constitutes and appoints with full power of substitution and revocation _E K Reid, of Chatham, Pittsylvania Co. Va_ her true and lawful attorney, to prosecute her claim and further declares that she has heretofore made _no_ application for (15) _a pension, but that she applied for Bounty land & rec'd a land warrant for 160 acres of land Cto. bq 084 dated the 18 June 1857"_ and that her residence is No. _____ street, city (or town) of _____ county of _Pittsylvania_, State of _Virginia_, and that her post-office address is _Shockoe Church Pittsylvania County Va_

ATTEST: _Richd White_ _Martha J Womack_ (Claimant's Signature.) _L Scruggs_

N. B.—All the blank spaces in this form must be carefully filled up in accordance with the instructions on the back hereof; and from the best information possessed, or obtainable, by the applicant.

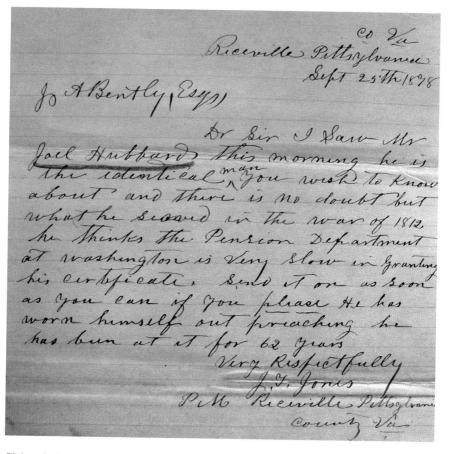

Claim of widow for pension for Martha Womack, widow of William Womack, who served in Captain Edward Carter's company of U.S. Cavalry. *National Archives and Records Administration, Chris Hanks.*

Opposite: Letter dated September 20, 1878, from Riceville in Pittsylvania County concerning the delay in the pension certificate for Joel Hubbard, a private in Captain John B. Royal's company in the 6th Regiment Virginia Militia. *National Archives and Records Administration, Chris Hanks.*

Records at the Bureau of Land Management in Washington show that Benjamin W.S. Cabell's own bounty land grants were in both Illinois and Wisconsin, totaling 160 acres. However, like most other veterans, he evidently sold the land to others.

As far as is known, at least six Pittsylvania soldiers died as a result of the war: John Shumate, Charles Nichols, William Parson, Hansen Regney, John Creasy and James Butcher. Two Pittsylvania County soldiers listed on the

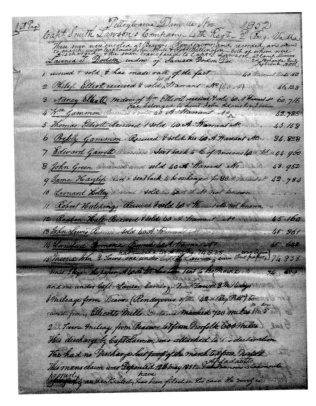

Above: Excerpt from a seventeen-page document, dated 1852, by General Benjamin W.S. Cabell to Edward A. Cabell, principal clerk at the land office in Washington, listing names of veterans relative to bounty land claims and allowances for travel. *National Archives and Records Administration, Chris Hanks.*

Left: Second excerpt from a document by General Benjamin W.S. Cabell concerning bounty land claims of War of 1812 veterans. *National Archives and Records Administration, Chris Hanks.*

roll of pensioners in 1883 received pensions due to wounds in the war—an injury of the abdomen in the case of William L. Fernald, and William G. Wynne suffered with a "g.s.w. of r. temple" (gunshot wound to right temple).

No doubt others from Pittsylvania County (including Danville) died or were wounded in that war. How many survivors remained in Pittsylvania County after the war is difficult to say. There are at least forty-five known graves of 1812 veterans in the county in thirty-five known cemeteries. However, the *Index of Pensioners* available through the National Archives indicates that there are an unknown number of veterans of the War of 1812 who died in the county and whose grave sites are not known.

While none of the original gravestones mentions the respective veteran's service, one in particular alludes to it. Daniel Coleman's gravestone gives his birth as June 7, 1768, and his death as April 8, 1860, near the beginning of the Civil War. It then reads, "His life was spent actively and usefully in his family neighborhood and County; much of it being devoted to his County both in a civil and military capacity, the duties of which he discharged with singular fidelity and efficiency."

Grave marker for Lieutenant Colonel Daniel Coleman, who served two tours of duty in the War of 1812. *Author's collection.*

Benjamin W.S. Cabell said of him in 1852, "Col. Daniel Coleman is now an aged man. In his boyhood he took part in the revolutionary struggle. In the war of 1812 he served two tours—and by his example animated his Countrymen, by his patriotic and gallant bearing." Daniel Coleman was likely the only soldier in Pittsylvania County to have served in both wars for American independence. Coleman lived to be ninety-two years old. Still, it would have been impossible for him or other Pittsylvania soldiers of the war to have seen the War of 1812's long-term results, given the perspective America now enjoys two hundred years later during the War of 1812 bicentennial.

Many soldiers had left the farm to march in defense of the ideals for

Cabin of Cornelius George, a private in Captain Tunstall Shelton's company, as it remains in 2014 at Pittsville community in Pittsylvania County. *Ginger Gentry.*

which America was founded and simply returned back home when their enlistments were over, without fanfare or accolades. They may have viewed their service as not of any unusual significance because it was sometimes brief and without confrontation with the enemy.

Yet Pittsylvania County soldiers who served in the Virginia Militia or in the U.S. Army would now be amazed at how their service propelled the United States into a new era of American history—an era that eventually led to the United States becoming the most powerful nation to ever exist on planet Earth.

Appendix I

WAR OF 1812 RESEARCH RELATED TO VIRGINIA SERVICEMEN

Records in state, university and local libraries and depositories are excellent sources of information in researching a War of 1812 ancestor. Local genealogical societies have family and local histories. Interlibrary loan of microfilm records as well as books also allows a researcher to borrow from other libraries. More local records can also be found at Clerk of Court Offices in various counties and cities, as well as in history centers, such as the Pittsylvania County History Center in Chatham, Virginia.

For Virginia ancestors, Stuart Butler's *Defending the Old Dominion* has a bibliographical section entitled "Archives and Manuscript Depositories." Butler, a former assistant chief of the Old Military and Civil Branch of the National Archives and Records Administration, has also written *A Guide to Virginia Militia Units in the War of 1812*, giving the command structure for the state and its counties, the companies of those counties called up for service and where they were sent. He has also published *Virginia Soldiers in the United States Army, 1800–1815*.

Nowadays, a great deal of research on the War of 1812 can be done online at various Internet websites. Sometimes the information is on the website directly. Otherwise, catalogues of libraries or depositories can be accessed online to find sources available. Examples are the Library of Virginia in Richmond and the University of Virginia Alderman and Small Special Collections Libraries in Charlottesville.

In researching the Virginia Militia, the records available at the Library of Virginia relating to the service of soldiers in that war are listed at http://www.

lva.virginia.gov/public/guides/rn19sold.htm. For example, the Library of Virginia has a list of forty thousand Virginia servicemen that can be accessed online, called "Index to War of 1812 Pay Rolls and Muster Rolls." This is not a complete list of all Virginia soldiers; about one-third of Virginia soldiers are not included. The only complete listing of Virginia soldiers in the War of 1812 is at the National Archives and Records Administration. The pension index can be accessed through Ancestry.com under "War of 1812 Pension Application Files Index, 1812–1815."

The National Archives and Records Administration website is the most extensive national source of U.S. government records on the war. *Prologue* magazine for the winter of 1991 has an article titled "Genealogical Records of the War of 1812" by Stuart Butler. The article discusses pension and bounty land warrant application files and military service records. The article also lists some National Archives publications that can assist a researcher in finding what sources are available in the archives.

One example of source material in the National Archives is the *Register of Enlistments in the U.S. Army 1798–1914*, available in NARA Microfilm Publication M233. Another NARA microfilm publication is M1856, which includes discharge certificates and other records of soldiers in the regular army from 1792 to 1815. This is part of Record Group 94, Records of the Adjutant General's Office, 1780s–1917. Information under this category can be accessed on the Internet (http://www.archives.gov/research/military/war-of-1812/1812-discharge-certificates/discharge-certificates.html).

Besides Ancestry.com, other valuable Internet sources of information on those who served in the War of 1812 include Fold3.com, Cyndislist.com, Familysearch.org and Archives.com. The Bureau of Land Management, under the "Land Patents" category, lists all the bounty land claims along with copies of the certificates (http://www.glorecords.blm.gov).

General sources of information about the war are found at the websites of historical groups, such as the Official War of 1812 Bicentennial Website, the National Society United States Daughters of 1812, the General Society of the War of 1812, the Society of the War of 1812 in Virginia and the Virginia Bicentennial of the American War of 1812 Commission.

Simply researching "the War of 1812" as a topic on an Internet search engine will lead to many more sources. Internet as well as library sources of information used in this book can be found in its bibliography.

Appendix II

PITTSYLVANIA COUNTY MILITIA

ORGANIZATION IN THE WAR OF 1812

42ⁿᵈ Regiment	101ˢᵗ Regiment
Lieutenant Colonel Daniel Coleman	Lieutenant Colonel Thomas H. Wooding
Major Jeremiah White	Major James Nowlin
Major Peter Wilson	Major John Bennett
Major Thomas Ragsdale	

PITTSYLVANIA MILITIA COMPANIES CALLED INTO SERVICE DURING THE WAR

INFANTRY
Lieutenant John Adams
Captain Thomas Clark
Lieutenant William Lewis
Captain William Linn
Lieutenant James Nance
Captain William Payne
Captain Thomas Ragsdale
Captain Tunstall Shelton

Captain Nathaniel Terry
Captain Nathaniel Wilson

ARTILLERY
Captain Samuel Calland
Captain George Townes

CAVALRY
Captain Edward Carter
Captain James Lanier

RIFLEMEN
Captain Dr. C. Williams

Source: Stuart Butler's *Guide to Virginia Militia Units in the War of 1812.*

Appendix III

SOME IMPORTANT DATES

IN THE WAR OF 1812

1812	Events
June 16	British "repeal" orders in Council
June 18	United States declares war against Britain
July 12	General Hull invades Upper Canada
July 17	Capture of Fort Mackinac
August 15	Fort Dearborn massacre
August 16	Surrender of Detroit
August 19	Capture of HMS *Guerriere*
October 13	Battle of Queenston Heights
December 26	Chesapeake Bay blockade declared

1813	
January 23	River Raisin massacre
March 3	Admiral Cockburn squadron in Bay
April 27	Battle of York
May 27	Battle of Fort George
June 1	HMS *Shannon* captures USS *Chesapeake*
June 13	British vessels repulsed at Burlington, Vermont

June 22	Battle of Craney Island
June 25	Attack on Hampton, Virginia
August 30	Fort Mims massacre
September 10	Battle of Lake Erie
October 5	Battle of the Thames
October 16	Battle of Leipzig/Napoleon defeated
October 26	Battle of Chateauguay
November 11	Battle of Chrysler's farm
December 10	Destruction of Newark in Canada

1814

March 27	Battle of Horseshoe Bend
March 30	Battle of Lacolle Mills
April 25	British extend blockade to New England
July 5	Battle of Chippawa
July 25	Battle of Lundy's Lane
August 8	Peace negotiations begin at Ghent
August 19	British land at Benedict, Maryland
August 24	Battle of Bladensburg
August 24	British burn Washington
August 28	British capture Alexandria
September 1	General Prevost moves toward Plattsburg
September 11	Battle of Plattsburg, New York
September 13	Bombardment of Fort McHenry
December 15	Federalists convene Hartford Convention
December 24	Treaty of Ghent signed in Belgium

1815

January 8	Battle of New Orlean

dates excerpted from Wikipedia.org

Appendix IV

LIST OF PENSIONERS ON THE ROLL, JANUARY 1883

Pittsylvania County, Virginia

98   LIST OF PENSIONERS.

VIRGINIA—Continued.

PITTSYLVANIA COUNTY.

No. of certifi-cate.	Name of pensioner.	Post-office ad-dress.	Cause for which pensioned.	Monthly rate.	Date of original al-lowance.
80, 918	Tash, Lucy	Berger's Store	widow 1812	$8 00	Dec., 1880
16, 544	McClanahan, Sallie A	do	do	8 00	Jan., 1879
17, 124	Parker, Permelia	do	do	8 00	Feb., 1879
21, 300	Barber, Tabitha A	do	do	8 00	Mar., 1879
24, 592	Shumaker, Jacob	do	surv. 1812.	8 00	Nov., 1878
12, 576	Lewis, Joseph	Brosville	do	8 00	Feb., 1872
23, 986	White, Clary	do	do	8 00	May, 1879
23, 700	Shelton, Anna	do	widow 1812	8 00	May, 1879
2, 562	Rogers, Lucy	Callands	do	8 00	Apr., 1872
31, 962	Hundley, Tabitha	do	do	8 00	Sept., 1881
16, 576	Blair, Clarissa W	do	do	8 00	Jan., 1879
21, 332	Grant, Mary Ann	do	do	8 00	Mar., 1879
25, 933	Wray, Nancy	do	do	8 00	July, 1879
25, 420	Pearson, Rachel	do	do	8 00	July, 1879
19, 169	Oakes, Sally	do	do	8 00	Feb., 1879
19, 916	Minter, Frances W	do	do	8 00	Mar., 1879
19, 681	Tucker, Sally	Chalk Level	do	8 00	Mar., 1879
18, 448	Tate, Nancy	do	do	8 00	Feb., 1879
17, 116	Shelton, Jane B	do	do	8 00	Feb., 1879
7, 105	Robertson, Nancy R. F	Chatham	do	8 00	July, 1875
8, 710	Ragsdale, Lucy B	do	do	8 00	Sept., 1875
19, 887	Robertson, Elizabeth	do	do	8 00	Mar., 1879
15, 146	Hutcherson, Elizab'h B	do	do	8 00	Jan., 1879
10, 065	Hardy, Evy	do	do	8 00	Nov., 1878
26, 954	Brumfield, Letitia	do	do	8 00	Sept., 1879
13, 272	Allen, Lavicy F	do	do	8 00	Dec., 1878
15, 473	Gaulding, Mary M	do	do	8 00	Jan., 1879
2, 227	Grubb, Polly	do	do	8 00	Mar., 1872
26, 940	Woodall, Elizabeth	do	do	8 00	Sept., 1879
17, 819	Mitcham, Mary F	do	do	8 00	Feb., 1879
8, 850	Keatts, Tempy C	do	do	8 00	Sept., 1875
2, 972	Lipford, Elizabeth	do	widow	8 00	Oct., 1868
13, 721	Suttle, John	do	surv. 1812.	8 00	Mar., 1872
20, 343	Jones, Mary S	Chestnut Level	widow 1812	8 00	Mar., 1879
22, 537	Wilburn, Sarah M	Clark's Level	do	8 00	Apr., 1879
25, 553	Sublett, Nancy	Danville	do	8 00	July, 1879
160, 205	Wynne, William G	do	g. s. w. of r. temple	8 00	June, 1880
15, 793	Thomas, William	do	surv. 1812.	8 00	Apr., 1879
30, 106	Fernald, William L	do	inj. to abdomen	4 00	Apr., 1872
170, 336	Gordon, M. E	do	widow	12 00	Dec., 1877
3, 413	Walker, Nancy	Hill Grove	widow 1812	8 00	July, 1872
22, 964	Simmons, Elizabeth J	Laurel Grove	do	8 00	Apr., 1879
13, 709	Dodson, Obedience	do	do	8 00	Dec., 1878
13, 977	Holt, Wilmoth	do	surv. 1812.	8 00	Dec., 1878
13, 364	Chaney, Elizabeth	do	widow 1812	8 00	Feb., 1879
18, 195	Colley, Sarah A	do	do	8 00	Feb., 1879
29, 361	White, Martha T	Malmaison	do	8 00	May, 1880
1, 068	Lewis, Polly	Malondsville	do	8 00	Mar., 1872
22, 537	Shelton, Eleanore P	Museville	do	8 00	Apr., 1879
15, 969	Dunn, Alley	Pleasant Gap	do	8 00	Jan., 1879
19, 684	Johnson, Letitia	do	do	8 00	Mar., 1879
5, 709	Dixon, Susan	Peytonsburgh	do	8 00	Oct., 1872
9, 318	Thompson, Ann D	Riceville	do	8 00	Sept., 1878
31, 421	Hubbard, Margaret H	do	do	8 00	Mar., 1881
20, 343	Lyon, Elienor H	Ringgold	do	8 00	Mar., 1879
19, 609	Davis, Martha H	do	do	8 00	Mar., 1879
19, 702	Townes, Sarah	do	do	8 00	Mar., 1879
2, 731	Billings, Calva	Sandy River	surv. 1812.	8 00	Jan., 1879
11, 440	Womack, Martha J	Shockoe Church	widow 1812	8 00	Nov., 1878
3, 179	Doss, Judith	Sycamore Station	do	8 00	July, 1872
2, 731	Door, Polly	do	do	8 00	May, 1872
12, 131	Mays, William	do	surv. 1812.	8 00	Feb., 1872
13, 442	Mayhue, Drury	do	do	8 00	Mar., 1872
1, 887	Pritchell, Sarah H	Whitmell	widow 1812	8 00	Mar., 1872
12, 355	Fuller, Mary	do	do	8 00	Nov., 1878

List of Pensioners on the roll, January 1883, vol. 5. *U.S. Pension Bureau, Government Printing Office, Washington, D.C.*

BIBLIOGRAPHY

General Sources for the War of 1812

Adams, James Truslow, Editor-in-Chief. *Dictionary of American History*. 2nd ed., rev. New York: Charles Scribner's Sons, 1940.

Armstrong, O.K. *The 15 Decisive Battles of the United States*. New York: Longmans, Green and Company, 1961.

Auchinleck, G. *A History of the War Between Great Britain and the United States During the Years 1812, 1813 and 1814*. Toronto: McClea and Company, 1855.

Badger, Barber. *The Naval Temple*. 2nd ed. Boston: self-published, 1816.

Bass, Barbara. "The War of 1812." *Halifax County, Virginia Bulletin* 28 (Fall 2013): 8–20.

Beard, Charles A., and Mary R. Beard. *A Basic History of the United States*. New York: Doubleday, Doran and Company, 1944.

———. *The Rise of American Civilization*. New York: Macmillan Company, 1940.

Beirne, Francis F. *The War of 1812*. Hamden, CT: Archon Books, 1965.

Bennett, William J. *America: The Last Best Hope*. Nashville, TN: Nelson Current, 2006.

Block, Jeremy. *Warfare in the Eighteenth Century*. Smithsonian History of Warfare Series. New York: HarperCollins, 1999.

Boneman, Walter R. *1812: The War that Forged a Nation*. New York: HarperCollins, 2004.

Brackenridge, H.M. *History of the Late War Between the United States and Great Britain.* Pittsburgh, PA: C.H. Kay and Company, 1844.

Brinkley, Alan. *The Unfinished Nation: A Concise History of the American People.* 4th ed. New York: McGraw-Hill, 2004.

Brock, Robert Alonzo, and Virgil Anson Lewis. *Virginia and Virginians.* Vol. 2. Richmond, VA: H.H. Hardesty, 1888.

Buel, Richard, Jr. *America on the Brink.* New York: Palgrave Macmillian, 2006.

Butler, Nicholas. "The Effect of the War of 1812 Upon the Consolidation of the Union." *Science* 10, no. 232 (July 1887): 30–31. Johns Hopkins University, Baltimore, Maryland. www.sciencemag.org.

Butterfield, Roger. *The American Past.* 2nd ed., rev. New York: Simon and Schuster, 1966.

Callo, Joseph F. "1812 Victory at Sea." *Military History* 27 (March 2011): 36–41.

Catton, Bruce, and William B. Catton. *The Bold and Magnificent Dream: America's Founding Years, 1492–1815.* Garden City, NY: Doubleday and Company, 1978.

Chamberlain, John. *The Enterprising Americans: A Business History of the United States.* New York: Harper and Row, 1974.

Chambers, John Whiteclay, ed. "The War of 1812." *American Military History.* New York: Oxford University Press, 1999.

Churchill, Winston S. *A History of the English Speaking Peoples.* Vol. 3, *The Age of Revolution.* New York: Dodd, Mead, and Company, 1957.

Collins, Mary Molnar, ed. "War Comes to the Chesapeake Bay." *National Society of the Daughters of 1812 Newsletter* 89 (August 2012): 8.

Commanger, Henry Steele, and Allan Nevins. *The Heritage of America.* Rev. ed. Boston: D.C. Heath and Company, 1949.

Cook, Jane Hampton. *American Phoenix.* Nashville, TN: Thomas Nelson, 2013.

Coxe, Tench. *A Statement of the Arts and Manufactures of the United States of America.* United States Census Office, Third Census. Washington, D.C.: U.S. Department of the Treasury, 1810.

Crain, Caleb. "Unfortunate Events." *New Yorker Magazine* 88 (October 22, 2012): 77–78.

Current, Richard N., and John A. Garraty, eds. *Words that Made American History: Colonial Times to 1820.* Boston: Little Brown and Company, 1962.

Dangerfield, George. *The Awakening of American Nationalism 1815–1828.* New York: Harper and Row, 1964.

Drake, Frederick C. "The Niagara Peninsula and the Naval Aspects of the War." *The Military in the Niagara Peninsula.* Ontario: Vanwell Publishers Limited, 1990.

Dupuy, R. Ernest, and Trever N. Dupuy. *The Encyclopedia of Military History from 3500 B.C. to the Present.* 2nd ed., rev. New York: Harper and Row, 1986.

Emerson, Edwin, Jr. *A History of the Nineteenth Century Year by Year.* New York: P.F. Collier and Son, 1902.

Emmerson, John Cloyd. *War in the Lower Chesapeake and Hampton Roads Areas, 1812–1815.* Accession no. 40754, Personal Papers Collection, Library of Virginia, Richmond, Virginia.

Ferling, John. *A Leap in the Dark: The Struggle to Create the American Republic.* New York: Oxford University Press, 2003.

Fleming, Thomas. "Dolly Madison Saves the Day." *Smithsonian Magazine* (March 2010): 50–56.

Foner, Eric. *Give Me Liberty: An American Story.* Vol. 1. 2nd ed. New York: W.W. Horton, 2009.

Foreman, Amanda. "America on Fire." *Smithsonian Magazine* (July–August, 2014): 37–40.

Fowler, William M., Jr. *Jack Tars and Commodores: The American Navy, 1783–1815.* Boston: Houghton-Mifflin, 1984.

Fredriksen, John C. *The United States Army in the War of 1812.* Jefferson, NC: McFarland & Company, 2009.

Fremont-Barnes, Gregory. *Nelson's Sailors.* Oxford, UK: Osprey, 2005.

Garraty, John A., and Peter Gay, eds. *The Columbian History of the World.* New York: Harper and Row, 1972.

George, Thomas R. *The George Family Record: Descendants of Colonel John George of Virginia.* Houston, TX: Hunter George Graphic Design, 1978.

Gerry, Elbridge, Jr. *The Diary of Elbridge Gerry, Jr.* New York: Brentanos, 1927.

Gilbert, Bil. "The Battle of Lake Erie." *Smithsonian Magazine* (January 1995): 24–34.

Gilje, Paul A. "Free Trade and Sailors' Rights: The Rhetoric of the War of 1812." *Journal of the Early Republic* 30 (Spring 2010): 1–23.

Glover, Michael. *The Napoleonic Wars: An Illustrated History, 1792–1815.* New York: Hippocrene Books, 1978.

Gordon, William. *A Compilation of Registers of the Army of the United States from 1815–1837.* Washington, D.C.: James C. Dunn, Printer, 1837.

Grant, John, and Ray Jones. *The War of 1812: A Guide to Battlefields and Historic Sites.* Buffalo: New York Public Broadcasting Association, 2011.

Hakim, Jay. *A History of US: A New Nation.* New York: Oxford University Press, 1993.

Harriss, Joseph. "Westward Ho!" *Smithsonian Magazine* (April 2003): 100–108.

Headley, J.T. *The Second War with England.* Vol. 2. New York: Charles Scribner, 1853.

Heidler, David S., and Jeanne T. Heidler. *Encyclopedia of the War of 1812.* Annapolis, MD: Naval Institute Press, 2004.

Hickey, Donald R. *The War of 1812: A Short History.* Urbana: University of Illinois Press, 1995.

Hobsbawn, Eric. *The Age of Revolution, 1789–1848.* New York: Vintage Books, 1962.

Horowitz, Tony. "Remember the Raisin." *Smithsonian Magazine* (June 2012): 28–35.

Jennings, Walter Wilson. *The American Embargo, 1807–1809, with Particular Reference to Its Effect on Industry.* Iowa City: University of Iowa, 1921.

Johnson, Eric E. "The Army's Register of Enlistments Pertaining to the War of 1812." *War Cry* 39 (Winter 2013): 7. General Society of the War of 1812.

Josephy, Alvin M., Jr. *The Indian Heritage of America.* New York: Alfred A. Knopf, 1973.

Kennedy, David, and Thomas Bailey, eds. *American Spirit: United States History as Seen by Contemporaries.* Vol. 1, *To 1877.* 10th ed. Boston: Houghton-Mifflin, 2002.

Langguth, A.J. *Union 1812: The Americans Who Fought the Second War of Independence.* New York: Simon and Schuster, 2006.

London Evening Star, September 1813.

Lord, Walter. *The Dawn's Early Light.* New York: W.W. Norton and Company, 1972.

Lossing, Benjamin John. *The Pictorial Field-Book of the War of 1812.* New York: Harper and Brothers, 1868.

Mahon, John K. *The War of 1812.* Gainesville: University of Florida Press, 1972.

Marden, Luis. "Old Ironsides." *National Geographic* (June 1997): 38–53.

Marquis, James. *The Life of Andrew Jackson.* Indianapolis, IN: Bobbs-Merrill Company, 1938.

Matloff, Maurice, gen. ed. *American Military History.* Army Historical Series. Washington, D.C.: U.S. Army, 1969.

Melton, Herman. *Picks, Tracks and Bateaux: Industry in Pittsylvania County, 1750–1950.* Lynchburg, VA: H.E. Howard, 1993.

Miers, Earl Schenk. *The American Story.* Kingsport, TN: Kingsport Press, 1956.

Miller, Joseph Lyon. *The Descendants of Capt. Thomas Carter, 1652–1912.* Bridgewater, VA: C.J. Carrier Company, 1967.

Morris, Richard B. *Encyclopedia of American History.* Rev. ed. New York: Harper and Row, 1961.

Mulhall, Jill K. *The War of 1812.* Reprint, 2011. Huntington Beach. CA: Teacher Created Materials, 2005.

Nash, Gary B. *Red, White, and Black: The Peoples of Early America.* 2nd ed. Englecliffs, NJ: Prentice-Hall, 1982.

National Park Service, U.S. Department of the Interior. "National Star-Spangled Banner Trail." Insert in *Bay Journeys* (Summer 2012). Chesapeake Media Services.

Niles, Hezekiah, ed. *Niles' Weekly Register,* March 7, 1812.

Powell, William H. *List of Officers in the Army of the United States from 1779–1900.* New York: H.R. Homersley and Company, 1900.

Registers of Enlistments in the U.S. Army, 1798–1914. NARA Microfilm Publication M233. Washington, D.C.: National Archives and Records Administration, n.d.

Rudanko, Juhani. "This Most Unnecessary, Unjust and Disgraceful War: Attacks on the Madison Administration in Federalist Newspapers During the War of 1812." *Journal of Historical Pragmatics* 12 (2011): 82–103.

Smelser, Marshall. *The Democratic Republic, 1801–1815.* New York: Harper and Row, 1968.

Smith, Page. *The Shaping of America.* Vol. 3. New York: McGraw-Hill, 1980.

Sneads, Scott S. *The Rockets' Red Glare: The Maritime Defense of Baltimore in 1814.* Centerville, MD: Tidewater Publishing, 1986.

Sundt, Wilbur A., and Richard R. Hobbs. *Naval Science: An Illustrated Text for the NJROTC Student.* Vol. 1. 2nd ed. Annapolis, MD: Naval Institute Press, 1987.

Swanson, Neil H. *The Perilous Fight.* New York: J.J. Little and Ives, 1945.

Thompson, David. *History of the Late War Between Great Britain and the United States of America.* Niagara, Upper Canada: T. Sewell, 1832.

Tindall, George Brown, and David E. Shi. *America: A Narrative History.* 7th ed. New York: W.W. Norton, 1984.

Tucker, Glenn. *Poltroons and Patriots.* Indianapolis, IN: Bobbs-Merrill, 1954.

Turner, Wesley B., ed. *The Military in the Niagara Peninsula.* St. Catherines, ON: Vanwell, 1990.

Tyler, Lyon G., ed. "Letter from Edward Coles to William C. Rives, January 21, 1856." *William and Mary Quarterly* 7 (January 1927): 162–65.

Villiers, Alan. *Men, Ships and Sea.* Washington, D.C.: National Geographic Society, 1973.

White, Patrick. *A Nation on Trial: America and the War of 1812.* New York: Wiley and Sons, 1965.

Whitley, Tyler. "Remembering the War of 1812." *Danville Register and Bee*, December 28, 2009.

Wolf, Joshua. "'To Be Enslaved or Thus Deprived': British Impressment, American Discontent, and the Making of the Chesapeake-Leopard Affair, 1803–1807." *War and Society Journal* 29 (May 2010): 1–19.

Woodard, W.E. *A New American History.* London: Faber and Faber Ltd., 1931.

Wood, Gordon. *Empire of Liberty: A History of the Early Republic, 1789–1815.* New York: Oxford University Press, 2009.

———. *Revolutionary Characters: What Made the Founders Different.* New York: Penguin Books, 2006.

SOURCES FOR THE WAR OF 1812 IN VIRGINIA

Aaron, Larry. "Daniel and Stephen Coleman: Patriot Brothers." *Pittsylvania Packet* 88 (Spring 2013): 14–17. Pittsylvania Historical Society.

Ancestry.com. "Some Soldiers from Pittsylvania County in the U.S. Army, 1800–1815." http://www.rootsweb.ancestry.com/~vapittsy/notes.htm.

Barbour, Governor James. Broadside regarding President Madison's proclamation of war, Richmond, 1812. Special Collections, University of Virginia, Charlottesville, Virginia.

Bolling, William. *Orderly Book in the War of 1812.* Accession no. 11138, Special Collections, University of Virginia, Charlottesville, Virginia.

Butler, Stuart. "Defending Norfolk." *Prologue* (Spring 2013): 1–18. http://www.archives.gov/publications/prologue/2013/spring/norfolk.pdf.

———. *Defending the Old Dominion: Virginia and Its Militia in the War of 1812.* Lanham, MO: University Press of America, 2013.

———. "Genealogical Records of the War of 1812." *Prologue* (Winter 1991): 1–5. http://www.archives.gov/publication/prologue/1991/winter/war-of-1812.html.

———. *A Guide to Virginia Militia Units in the War of 1812.* 2nd ed. Athens, GA: New Papyrus Publishing, 2011.

———. "War of 1812 Began with Close Votes." *Richmond-Times Dispatch*, June 3, 2012.

Clement, Maud. *The History of Pittsylvania County, Virginia.* Lynchburg, VA: J.P. Bell, 1929.

———. Maud Clement Papers. Special Collections, University of Virginia, Charlottesville, Virginia.

Coleman, Daniel. Letter to James Breckinridge, October 8, 1814. Accession no. 19876, Personal Papers Collection, Library of Virginia, Richmond, Virginia.

Coles, Edward. "Edward Coles to Dolly Madison." October 5, 1812 (abstract). Founders Online, National Archives. http://founders.archives. gov./documents/Madison/03-05-02-0276. Also in the Papers of James Madison, Presidential Series, vol. 5, July 10, 1812–February 7, 1813, J.C.A. Stagg et als.

Coles, John. John Coles Papers, 1806–1844. Accession no. 1606, Special Collections, University of Virginia, Charlottesville, Virginia. http://search.lb.virginia.edu/catalog.

Coles, Walter I, and Elbridge Gerry Jr. Letters Received by the Adjutant General's Office, March 30, 1812; February 28, 1814; June 30, 1814; December 14, 1814. Record Group 94, National Archives and Records Administration, Washington, D.C.

———. Letters to Catherine Coles in Pittsylvania County, 1812–1815. Transcribed September 13, 1812; December 22, 1812; April 26, 1813; June 15, 1813. Private collection of Walter Coles IV, Coles Hill, Pittsylvania County.

Coles, William Bedford. *The Coles Family of Virginia*. Baltimore, MD: Gateway Press, 1931.

Douthat, James L. *Roster of the War of 1812, Southside, Virginia: For the Twenty-Six Counties in This Area of Virginia*. Signal Mountain, TN: Mountain Press, 2007.

Durkee, Cutler. "The Real Seawolf." *Smithsonian Magazine* 34 (December 2003): 74–76.

Flournoy, H.W. *Calendar of Virginia State Papers*. Vols. 9–10. Richmond: Virginia State Library, 1890, 1892.

Gerry and Coles Family Papers. Original letters from Walter Coles I and Elbridge Gerry Jr. to Catherine Coles of Pittsylvania County, Virginia, September 25, 1812; June 14, 1814; October 17, 1813; November 21, 1813; March 9, 1814; September 4, 1814; February 27, 1815. Huntington Library, San Marino, California.

Gordon, W.J., Acting Adjutant, 3rd Rifle Regiment, U.S. Army. "Deserters." *Raleigh Minerva*, February 10, 1815. From U.S. Genweb Archives. Original source is Military Records of North Carolina Archives. http://www.genrecords.net/ncfiles.

Grasty, Philip. Philip Grasty to Governor James Barbour, May 20, 1812. Executive Letters Received, Record Group 3, Library of Virginia, Richmond, Virginia.

Hairston, Samuel, Jr. Letter dated August 4, 1813. Letters Received by the Adjutant General's Office, Record Group 94, National Archives and Records Administration, Washington, D.C.

———. Letter to George Hairston, November 7, 1812. Robert Hairston Papers, 1799–1862. Davis Library, Southern Historical Collection, University of North Carolina–Chapel Hill, North Carolina.

———. Letter to Secretary of War John Armstrong, August 10, 1813. Letters Received by the Adjutant General's Office, Record Group 94, National Archives and Records Administration, Washington, D.C.

Hallahan, John M. *The Battle of Craney Island: A Matter of Credit.* Portsmouth, VA: St. Michael's Press, 1986.

Hanks, Chris. "The Cabell Document." Includes description of letter from Benjamin W.S. Cabell to Edward Cabell, November 26, 1852. Pension Records in National Archives, Washington, D.C.

Hanks, Chris, researcher. Grave markers and notes for various veterans of the War of 1812 buried in Pittsylvania County. http://pittsylvaniacountyhistory.com.

———. War of 1812 pension records. Various Pittsylvania County veterans' files from National Archives in Washington, D.C.

Huckabee, Malcolm, ed. "Col. Daniel Coleman 1768–1860 Obituary" by General Benjamin W.S. Cabell in the *Danville Appeal*, May 2, 1860. In *Piedmont Lineages* 34 (August 2012): 9–10. Virginia–North Carolina Genealogical Society.

Hume, Edgar Erskine. "Letters Written During the War of 1812 by the British Naval Commander in American Waters (Admiral Sir David Milne)." *William and Mary Quarterly* 10, no. 4 (October 1930): 280–99.

Ingram, Sonja. "Historic Fearn Property." *Danville Historical Society Newsletter* 6, no. 4 (November 2012): 2.

Journal of the Executive Proceedings of the United States Senate. Vol. 2. Washington, D.C.: Duff Green, 1828.

Ledgers of Payments to U.S. Pensioners under Acts of Congress 1818 through 1858 from Records of the Office of the Third Auditor of the Treasury. Microfilm Publication T718. National Archives and Records Administration, Washington, D.C.

List of Pensioners on the Roll January 1883. Vol. 5. U.S. Pension Bureau. Washington, D.C.: Government Printing Office, 1883.

Lyman, Myron E. "3828 War of 1812 Veteran Burials in Virginia Listed by Veterans and Cemetery Locations." Society of the War of 1812 in Virginia, 2009. 1812va.org.

Lyman, Myron E., and William W. Hankins. "Encounters with the British in Virginia During the War of 1812." Society of the War of 1812 in Virginia, 2008–9. 1812va.org.

Manuscript Maps of Military Installations on Craney Island, Virginia in the War of 1812. Accession no. 1643, Special Collections, University of Virginia, Charlottesville.

McGhee, Lucy Kate, comp. *Virginia Pension Abstracts of the Revolutionary War, War of 1812, and Indian Wars.* Washington, D.C., n.d.

Mitchell, Henry, and Sarah Mitchell. "Dolly Madison and the Coles Family of Virginia." Victorian Villa. www.victorianvilla.com.

Mitchell, Sarah E. "Pittsylvania Veterans of the War of 1812 Still Living in 1883." *Pittsylvania Packet* 71 (Winter 2009): 14–17. Pittsylvania Historical Society, Chatham, Virginia.

Nance, James. "James Nance His Book," family register. Pittsylvania County History. pittsylvaniacountyhistory.com/james-nance.

Newfield, Gareth. "Anatomy of Atrocity: Crimes of the Independent Companies of Foreigners in North America, 1813." *War of 1812 Magazine* 10 (October 2008). http://www.napoleon-series.org/military/Warof1812/2008/Issue10/c_Foreigners.html.

Pay Rolls of the Militia Entitled to Land Bounty under the Act of Congress of Sept. 28, 1850. Library of Virginia, Richmond, Virginia.

Peter Wilson Papers, 1773–1965; 1986. Davis Library, Southern Historical Collection, University of North Carolina–Chapel Hill, North Carolina.

Pittsylvania County Clerk's Office. Court records, vol. 15, 1812–1815. Chatham, Virginia.

"Pocket" Plantation, 1748–1861: Pittsylvania County, Virginia. Accession no. 2027. Davis Library, Southern Historical Collection, University of North Carolina–Chapel Hill, North Carolina.

Pratt, Julius W. *Expansionists of 1812.* New York: Macmillan, 1925. Reviewed in *Virginia Historical Magazine* 33 (1925).

Virginia Governor Barbour Executive Papers, 1812–1814. Accession no. 41557. State government records collection, Library of Virginia, Richmond, Virginia.

Virginia Militia in the War of 1812: From Rolls in the Auditor's Office at Richmond. Baltimore, MD: Genealogical Publishing Company, 2001.

Virginia Militia Muster and Payrolls, 1812–1815. Accession no. 36881. State government records collection, Library of Virginia, Richmond, Virginia.

"Virginia Militia, War of 1812, Orderly Books." Accession no. 38-728-a. Tracy W. McGregor Library, Special Collections, University of Virginia Library, Charlottesville, Virginia.

Additional Website Resources

Canadian Register of Historic Places, Quebec, Canada. "War of 1812 Timeline." http://www.historicplaces.ca/en/pages/33_1812.aspx.

Digital Scholarship Lab, University of Richmond. "Reasons for the War of 1812." History Engine, Tools for Collaborative Education and Research, 2008–9. historyengine.richmond.edu/episodes/view/4574.

The Discriminating General. "The War of 1812." www.warof1812.ca.

Mariners Museum, Norfolk, Virginia. "Birth of the U.S. Navy." Prelude to the War of 1812. http://www.marinersmuseum.org/site/micro/usnavy/08/08a.htm.

Military Society of the War of 1812. "The War of 1812." http://militarysocietywar1812.com/history.html.

PBS—War of 1812. "Military Medicine in the War of 1812." http://www.pbs.org/wned/war-of-1812/essays/military-medicine.

Smithsonian Institution. "A Nation Emerges." www.npg.si.edu/exhibit/1812.

Thomas Jefferson's Monticello. Coles, John, Edward Cole and Isaac Coles. http://www.monticello.org/site/research-and-collections.

Virginia Places. "Craney Island." http://www.virginiaplaces.org/transportation/craney.html.

INDEX

V

W

Y

ABOUT THE AUTHOR

Larry Aaron is an associate editor of *Evince* news magazine and a local historian from Danville, Virginia. He has received first-place awards from the Virginia Press Association and is the author of eight books, including *Keppy's War*, *The Race to the Dan* and *Aaron, Arnn, Aron Ancestors of Pittsylvania County, Virginia*. Among his previously published books are two with The History Press: *The Wreck of the Old 97*, which was nominated for the Non-Fiction Prize in the Library of Virginia's annual literary competition for 2011, and *Pittsylvania County: A Brief History*.

Aaron graduated from Virginia Tech with a BS in biology and also has earned BRE, MDiv and Doctor of Ministry degrees. Among his accomplishments, he was invited to speak on the famous country ballad "The Wreck of the Old 97" at the International Conference of Country Music in Nashville, Tennessee. Presently, he is state historian of the Virginia Society, Sons of the American Revolution, and state chaplain of the War of 1812 Society in Virginia. He lives with his wife, Nancy, in Danville, Virginia.

Visit us at
www.historypress.net

....

This title is also available as an e-book